FAIRWAY
TO
HELL

FAIRWAY TO

HELL

AROUND THE WORLD IN 18 HOLES

FRANZ LIDZ

FIRST EDITION

10 9 8 7 6 5 4 3 2 1

ESPN
BOOKS
a division of
ESPN publishing

The following were originally published in slightly different form in *Sports Illustrated* and are reprinted
courtesy of *Sports Illustrated:* "Deadly Bolts" by Franz Lidz, April 23, 2007, Copyright © 2007. Time Inc.
All reserved; "To Honor The Father" by Franz Lidz, June 19, 2006, Copyright © 2006. Time Inc. All reserved; "Stealth Bomber" by Franz Lidz, July 18, 2006, Copyright © 2006. Time Inc. All reserved; "For the
People" by Franz Lidz, May 8, 2006, Copyright © 2006. Time Inc. All reserved; "House Money" by Franz
Lidz, September 19, 2005, Copyright © 2005. Time Inc. All reserved; "Day Job" by Franz Lidz, August 1,
2005, Copyright © 2005. Time Inc. All reserved; "Skin Game" by Franz Lidz, March 28, 2005, Copyright ©
2005. Time Inc. All reserved; "Just Doo It" by Franz Lidz, Nov. 8, 2005, Copyright © 2005. Time Inc. All
reserved; "Subway Series" by Franz Lidz, June 11, 2001, Copyright © 2001. Time Inc. All reserved;
"Swingin' Singles" by Franz Lidz, April 2, 2001, Copyright © 2001. Time Inc. All reserved; "Fat Accompli"
by Franz Lidz, August 14, 2000, Copyright © 2000. Time Inc. All reserved; "Hidden Talent," by Franz Lidz,
August 23, 1999, Copyright © 1999. Time Inc. All reserved; "A Swingin' Affair" by Franz Lidz, July 13,
1998, Copyright © 1998. Time Inc. All reserved; "Neither New Nor Improved" by Franz Lidz, July 28,
1997, Copyright © 1997. Time Inc. All reserved; "Different Strokes" by Franz Lidz, December 23, 1996,
Copyright © 1996. Time Inc. All reserved; "Ice Capades" by Franz Lidz, August 19, 1996, Copyright ©
1996. Time Inc. All reserved; "Veteran in Training" by Franz Lidz, December 11, 1995, Copyright © 1995.
Time Inc. All reserved; "Holy Cow, Robert!" by Franz Lidz, December 5, 1994, Copyright © 1994. Time
Inc. All reserved; "The Putt-Putt Chronicles" by Franz Lidz, November 3, 1994, Copyright © 1994. Time
Inc. All reserved; "'I Am Not a Flake" by Franz Lidz, March 9, 1992, Copyright © 1992. Time Inc. All re-
served; "In Golf, Recycling" by Franz Lidz, May 14, 1990, Copyright © 1990. Time Inc. All reserved;
"Heavy Metal Golfers Find Peace And Quiet" by Franz Lidz, October 27, 1986, Copyright © 1986. Time
Inc. All reserved; "Good 'Ol Charlie Schulz" by Franz Lidz, December 23, 1985, Copyright © 1985. Time
Inc. All reserved; "Mickey Wittman Swells With Pride" by Franz Lidz, October 10, 1983, Copyright ©
1983. Time Inc. All reserved.

The following were originally published in slightly different form in *Travel & Leisure Golf* and are
reprinted courtesy of *Travel & Leisure Golf:* "Llamas—As Caddies, They're Not Too Great"; "The Nastiest
Golf Course on Earth."

For

Isolde Motley
and the Ipaktchi brothers, Iradj and Kouros

Jerry Renner, requiescat in pace

*"When you are in the last ditch
with your back to the wall,
there is nothing left to do but sing."*

- SAMUEL BECKETT -

CONTENTS

FOREWORD

My favorite golfer has a 24 handicap. His name is Bill Krackomberger, and none of Atlantic City's other creatures looks quite like him. At six feet and 425 pounds, "Krackman" is roughly square. He weighs about 250 pounds more than the typical hacker, 200 more than his chunkiest playing partner, and 150 more than the average New Jersey household. His eyes are hooded slits; his teeth are splinters; his jowls are endowed with pockets of flab so thick, they droop almost to his ankles. The belly of Krackman is independently suspended, a nose cone of blubber cantilevered out from a perilously low-slung belt. On the raw public links of Galloway, it sits in a succession of garish sweaters. The electric-burgundy Pringles, he buys at Rochester Big & Tall on South Maryland Parkway in Las Vegas, a mere 5,472 miles from Savile Row. His other favorite outfitter is Casual Male Big & Tall. "At Casual Male," he says, "I buy clothes only from the George Foreman line." Very loyal is Krackman.

Red Smith liked to remind sanctimonious press box colleagues that sports are games played by kids. In Krackman's case, that dictum has come true with a vengeance. The Goliath of Galloway feels he's never more himself than when he's in touch with the 10-year-old who resides within. He whacks and thwacks through the rough with a schoolboy's exuberance, his voice as loud as his custom Sansabelts (the ones that look like Japanese TV test patterns). At a time when the pros tend to be solemn automatons who look as if they have been dressed by their mothers, Krackman is an authentic of the sort golf once produced in abundance. And if today his breed seems like an endangered species, that may be a measure of the diminished quality of modern life.

Until the mid-18th century, golf was a disorganized sport dominated by the Krackmans of the world. They played for legs of mutton, haunches of venison, firkins of claret, port, and whiskey. Then one day in 1744, some young urban professionals in Scotland formed the Honourable Company of Edinburgh Golfers. The prize of their first tournament—the Silver Club trophy—was won, naturally enough, by local surgeon John Rattray. Alas, after successfully defending his title the following year, Rattray was roused from his bed to be surgeon general of Bonnie Prince Charlie's army at the Battle of Prestonpans. A year later he was taken prisoner at Culloden and condemned to the gallows. It was only through the intervention of Scotland's senior judge, himself a fellow Gentleman Golfer, that Rattray was released from prison in time to play in the 1748 competition. He thus became the first golfer ever to benefit from being a member of a good club.

Ever since, golf has been a resonant byword for well-padded bourgeois complacency. These days, in the age of Tiger Inc., it is an essentially joyless business with too much character and not enough characters. The best-known courses have been tarted up to attract the coddled duffer accustomed to immaculate, unnatural conditions.

And the pro tours are stuffed with navel-entranced country clubbers stamped from the same dull mold. They are moderate. They are analytical. They are personality-free. They are forever shaking hands, exchanging treacly smiles, and extolling the life-affirming qualities of cleat tightening. "It is my goal to play 72 holes without changing the expression on my face," PGA Tour veteran Jack Renner once said. "If Ben Hogan could do it, I can too." After hearing this, I wished on Renner the same fate Celia intended for her beau in P.G. Wodehouse's uproarious golf story *The Salvation of George Mackintosh*: death by mashie niblick.

Wodehouse was golf's Shakespeare, its master comedian and tragedian. At an impressionable age, I fell in love with his *Golf Omnibus*, a British Open of loopy links yarns. A master of *le mot juste* who always zigged where you expected him to zag, Wodehouse confected a cloudless Neverland in which butterflies loaf languidly, plots tangle exquisitely, and love ("He folded her in his arms, using the interlocking grip") invariably triumphs over a 15 handicap. Golf and romance are constants. "I doubt if golfers should fall in love," muses one member. "I have known it to cost men 10 shots per medal round."

Within a P.G.-rated world, everyone is slightly ridiculous but never contemptible. Wodehouse had great affection for golfing's "goofs," those "unfortunate beings who have allowed this noblest of sports to ... eat into their souls." They live—or more properly, goof off—with an obstinate diffidence, in thrall to that ancient and wretched game. Wodehouse once said he suspected that golf was less a microcosm of life than life was a microcosm of golf. To his callow dingbat Bertie Wooster it was a raison d'etre, the alpha and the omega. Bertie's highest ambition in life is to do the dogleg hole at the Squashy Hollow Golf Club in under double figures. "Really bad golf," he reckons, "is a thing which purges the soul, and a man becomes better and broader from watching it."

In this spirit of purgation then, with the noble aim of making us all better and broader human beings, I have sought out subjects who best fit the Wodehousian ideal. Cow farmer-turned-Seniors Tour phenom Robert Landers had the haggard, careworn look of the Wodehouse naïf who "like a Borgia has suddenly remembered that he has forgotten to shove cyanide in the consommé, and the dinner-gong due at any moment." John Hardy, the podgiest swatter at the Fatty Open—that annual celebration of golf and gluttony in New Haven at which no one has ever hit it thin— recalled the lovably inept Wodehouse boulevardier who "looked as if he had been poured into his clothes and had forgotten to say, 'when.' " And the intelligence of a certain E-lister with whom I mingled at the Frank Sinatra Celebrity Classic was (to borrow from The Master) "somewhat lower than that of a backward clam—a clam, let us say, which has been dropped on its head when a baby."

While scouring the world for odd golf shrines and even odder golf shriners, I made pit stops in a nudist colony, a heavy metal rock concert, a llama farm, a transcendental airport for yogic flying, my own adolescence, and a dozen more of the world's little purgatories. I looped the globe as if it were a golf course, making catastrophic detours to shaggy doglegs on several continents. In all, I hit 18 of golf's most remote watering holes, from the parched plains of Toco, Texas, to the tangled sub-Saharan bush of Chililabombwe, Zambia.

For those readers without a scorecard, that's 18 holes, 18 chapters—19 if you count the account of how golf saved my life; 20 including the appreciation of Pebble Beach irregular Charles Schulz. Okay, make that 21—I neglected to include my meditation on the ordure of the day. And yeah, technically, the chapters on glacier golf, botflies, range balls, lightning, eminent domain, and the rocket-powered golf cart make, what, nearly 30? So let's just drop the whole chapters/holes idea, shall we?

Along the way I met gaggles of goofs—in varying sizes, shapes, and stages of sobriety—each in touch with a kind of pure, childlike joy; each infused with a Wodehousian sense of the elegant and the absurd.

Golf in a nutshell.

FAIRWAY TO HELL

BILOXI, MISSISSIPPI

"**J**udas Priest!"

The screaming 15-year-old caddy hasn't just been bonked by an errant 9-iron shot. He's caught sight of two golfers on the 3rd green at Hickory Hill Country Club near Biloxi, Mississippi. The pair play on.

"Judas Priest!" the caddy repeats, approaching the green. "You guys really play golf?"

Ignoring the gallery, one golfer sinks a 12-foot putt. The other whirls around to face the teenager. "Yes," he replies. "But we do worship the devil at night."

The putter is Glenn Tipton, and his partner is K. K. Downing, both on the near side of 60. They're the lead guitarists in Judas Priest, Britain's mock-satanic heavy metal band. In real life, Downing and Tipton feel more passion for golf than sympathy for the devil. They play the game as often as three times a week when on tour. Both claim to shoot in the low 80s, though when pressed Tipton admits, "There are times when the scorecard blows away."

They're such golf maniacs that they sometimes set up a putting green backstage. "We're totally into it," says Downing. "The yardages, which ball to use, who's cheating ..."

None of the middle-aged backers working their way around Hickory Hill recognizes them. But by the time the twosome reaches the 7th hole, every adolescent boy in Biloxi who's ever tried on a studded dog collar—and the number would surprise you—is hiding out in the bunkers, ready to ambush Tipton and Downing for autographs.

A kid in a HELL-BENT FOR LEATHER T-shirt pops out from behind a tree: "I went to your concert! Boy, were you loud! I mean, you were good, but boy, were you *loud*."

Downing and Tipton are in Biloxi for the 77th concert of their 80-date North American tour. Onstage, amid belching smoke and singer Rob Halford's thumbscrew screaming, the pair strut, swagger, and carry on like point men in a mutant army looking for Mad Max. Their brain-bludgeoning guitar riffs roar like Formula One racing cars, terrifying parents from Copenhagen to Carmel.

In the less permissive '80s, an enraged Tipper Gore, wife of the former vice president, had the lyrics of the band's song "Eat Me Alive" read to a startled Senate Commerce Committee. "We've written hundreds of songs, and she has to pick on that," says Downing. "Of course, it was a good one to pick on."

Seems that everyone from parents groups to chain stores loves to pick on Judas Priest. Even the news of being banned from Malaysia doesn't surprise them.

That has only given the guitarists more time to tee it up. They took up the game about 20 years ago, when their counterparts in Def Leppard, another band in the heavy metallurgical mold, challenged them to a game. "They thrashed us," says Downing. "But we got the bug."

At first they went to great lengths to conceal their new addiction. The sport might be fine for midlevel executives at U.S. Steel, but for heavy metal rockers, it presents something of a PR problem. "We felt golf could be detrimental to our leather-and-studs image," says Downing. "But then we thought, if word gets out, parents might decide that perhaps we're not bad chaps after all.

"On the other hand, if they hear Judas Priest is hacking down the fairway, they may assume we attach six-inch nails to our clubs before swinging them."

Not so. Downing and Tipton take a genteel approach to the game. They wear subdued polo shirts and slacks, and white golf shoes with fringed tongues. They scrupulously observe golf etiquette, gently tamping their divots back into place.

Golf, Downing and Tipton say, is a calm counterpoint to the hectic pace of life on the road. Still, the silence of the links occasionally unnerves them. "I've played stadiums before a hundred thousand people," Downing says. "And yet when the greenskeepers turn their tractors off and wait for me to take my swing, I get as nervous as hell."

On this afternoon, the weather is fittingly theatrical: portentous black clouds, sudden shafts of sunlight, gusts of chilly air. "It's all part of heavy metal golf," Tipton says. "Usually, before teeing it up, a bolt of lightning comes down and scorches the earth: JUDAS PRIEST KEEP OFF."

Tipton is still reeling from a night of rock and revelry. At the 8th hole, he slices his drive into the deep rough. But pulling out one of his heaviest metals—a 3-iron—he reaches the green in two. "I struck it a little better," he says groggily. "I think my mind's clearing a bit."

The sky, however, is growing increasingly ominous. A rainstorm moves in and washes out the game. After nine holes, Downing has a 40. Tipton's scorecard has blown away.

They ride the cart back to the clubhouse. "Hey, man," yells a bystander. "Y'all Judas?"

"No," says Downing wearily. "He's among the disciples behind us."

FAT ACCOMPLI

NEW HAVEN, CONNECTICUT

A 5-iron in one hand, two sticks of pepperoni in the other, Greg Laugeni clomps around the parking lot at the Yale Golf Club, chewing the fat with his partner, John Hardy. Considering that Laugeni weighs 390 pounds and Hardy 530 pounds, there's a lot of fat to chew.

Laugeni plops down at the nurse's station and has his blood pressure taken. When the nurse tells him it's 158 over 120, he nearly plotzes. "If you're right," says the 36-year-old contractor, "I should have died nine days ago!"

"Eight," corrects the nurse.

Hardy's turn. A look of incredulity spreads across the nurse's face. "You're 200 over 100!" she says, flicking and reflicking the gauge with her finger. "This may be a world record. Have you ever had a cholesterol count?"

"Cholesterol!" Hardy harrumphs. "Lady, with blood pressure this high, what's the difference?"

Hardy and Laugeni were in New Haven for the Fatty Open, an annual celebration of golf and gluttony at which Big Bertha could be a groupie. The one-day, two-ball, four-player scramble is perhaps the only sporting event with a weight *minimum*: Entrants are penalized 25 cents for every pound they come in under 250.

Before play began, each of the 88 golfers was required to sit on a meat scale rigged to a forklift. Hardy, Laugeni, and the rest of their foursome didn't wind up owing a penny. In fact, they had a quarter-ton of breathing room—in their case, heavy breathing room.

Weighing in at 1,520 pounds, they took the prize for total heft (each of them was awarded a 50-pound block of butter, a 24-pack of toilet paper, and a chocolate chip cookie the size of a manhole cover) as easily as Hardy took the prize for highest blood pressure (10 pounds of bacon and a George Foreman grill. Hardy was only modestly miffed that the grill didn't come with a car adapter).

"I'll never get to be the fattest golfer in the Fatty Open," groused 265-pounder Mike Guerra. "Hardy makes me look like a pencil neck."

Called Hardware during his days as a defensive tackle at Ole Miss, Hardy is a veritable Victoria Falls of flab. The energy broker's gut is so vast that you could hide *Oliver* Hardy in his navel. Compared to him, ex-offensive tackle Laugeni, who overheated so often at Holy Cross that he was dubbed The Radiator, is a mere cascade.

The weight of the quartet's other two members—315-pound Brian "The Happy Tuna" Marcucio and 285-pound Wayne "Cracker" Ritzy—barely equaled that of Hardy's appendages. "It's flattering to be part of this group," said Marcucio while posing for a team photo. "This is the first picture ever taken of me in which I didn't have to try to look thin."

The remainder of the Fatty field was larded with plump plumbers, stout salesmen, portly private eyes, roundish restaurateurs, fleshy florists, and one overnourished undertaker. "We need an undertaker on-site," said Dave Horton, the club's chubby chef. "Just in case."

Horton came up with the idea for the Fatty Open in 1997. He was out on the links when one of his golfing buddies said: "Will you look at all the porkers out here!"

"You know, you're right," said Horton. "Let's have a tournament for them."

Displaying the perseverance of his namesake from the Dr. Seuss classic, Horton somehow cajoled the directors of the renowned 80-year-old club into hosting the fatfest. The proceeds help fund research for a Yale-New Haven Hospital study of—what else?—eating disorders.

"It's less a tournament than a tailgate," Horton says. "A bunch of large players hacking around, feasting all day, having fun. It's not really about golf. It's about food."

Horton provides lots of it: Besides a buffet lunch and dinner, each golfer is entitled to a gift bag that includes a Slim Jim, Oreos, and a pack of Rolaids. Snack bars at the

9th and 13th holes are stocked with candy, cookies, chips, and beer. Barbecued franks and burgers await players at the 3rd hole, where hitting closest to the buffet table (about a 265-yard drive) gets you a microwave oven. (In the event of a tie, the ball closest to the mayonnaise wins. Last year, Ritzy claimed the prize after his ball landed in a hot dog roll.)

Sadly, not one of the gorging golfers was female. Horton had hoped for a women's division, but so far, he hasn't had a single taker. "Women get a little nutty about their weight," he reasons. "When guys get big and fat and sloppy, they don't care."

Laugeni is living proof. Polishing off the "Please See Fatty, Page B-2 Porterhouse Steak" at Don Shula's Restaurant in Miami Beach earned him a spot in the 64-ouncer Hall of Fame. Tears welled up in Laugeni's eyes when he recalled the Zen-like night in college when he became "at one" with 12 lobsters, 72 jumbo shrimp, 14 eight-ounce steaks, two slices of prime rib ("not slabs—you know, thin"), a pineapple, and three bottles of wine. "My roommate watched me in awe," he said. "Then he went into the bathroom and threw up."

These days, Laugeni watches what he eats. It's not that he eats any less, mind you; he just watches it. And it was hard not to stare at him tooling around the course in his cart while he clutched two wieners, three packs of Twizzlers, six bags of M&M's, and a Diet Coke.

Not surprisingly, Laugeni and Hardy were assigned separate carts. "This course is very hilly, and if these two were in the same vehicle, I'd be a little nervous about the brakes," explained Horton. "Nine hundred and twenty pounds in one cart is a lot of beef. Remember John Candy in *Stripes*: During basic training, he started running and couldn't stop until he reached the next state."

Not unexpectedly, on the par 4 1st hole, Hardy hits the ball just a little bit chunky. The low liner makes straight for a flock of Canadians wading in Griest Pond.

"The geese are running!" shouts Marcucio.

"They ought to be," Ritzy replies. "John looks like he's hungry."

Ritzy's opening shot carries a corner of the water hazard before it breaches the fairway. His follow-up bounds across the rippling putting green, and stops five feet from the cup.

When Laugeni sinks a four-foot putt for a birdie, he and Hardy celebrate by banging bellies like *Fantasia* hippos. The force of the collision causes Macucio and Ritzy to duck for cover and office buildings to sway in Bridgeport, 60 miles away.

"Who won?" asks Ritzy after getting the all-clear.

"Nobody," says Hardy. "It wasn't mean. There was nothing but love in that bump."

As the portly procession plods uphill to the next hole, a fellow fatty passes from the opposite direction. "If you see a Maxfli in the rough," he says, "pick it up for me, will ya?"

"Sorry," says Laugeni. "I haven't been able to bend since 1989." The big question isn't whether he'll last through 18 holes, but whether he'll *live* through them.

By the time they reach the 4th hole, the drizzle has turned to a steady downpour. Their clothes are soaked. Laugeni tugs at the sleeves of the black shirt he wore to "slenderize" himself and expounds on slices.

"You wanna know what makes a really good pizza?" he says. "I'll tell you what makes a really good pizza: the sauce, just the sauce. That's how you tell a really good pie. The sauce."

He champions the sausage special at Zuppardi's. "They make their own hot sausage on the premises and throw it on the pie in clumps," he says. "Nothing beats grabbing a piece of Zuppardi's pie and eating their clumps."

Hardy demurs. "Haven't you ever had the white clam pizza at Pepe's?" he asks. "Clams, garlic, and a layer of mozzarella. No tomato sauce."

"Pepe's? What about Sally's? I'd settle for any of their bacon, mushroom, and pepper pies. On second thought, hold the peppers. I'm not a big peppers guy. If I'm in the mood for a little twist, I ask them to toss in a few dollops of ricotta."

Hardy is salivating like one of Pavlov's pups. "I think I'd take Pepe's pizza over sex," he says. "The wait outside is an hour and a half."

Which is only slightly longer than the delay at the snack shed at the 9th tee. The rain falls fatly as they gaze out at the famous green, which keeps going and going and going for maybe 50 yards. Split down the middle by an eight-foot swale, it's about the size of the double green on the Old Course at St. Andrews. In other words, it's almost as big as Hardy's appetite.

"My game is totally screwed up," he sighs. "All I can think about is that pizza."

The other three agree: It's time to pack it in and start packing it on. "After this hole, I think we're done," sputters the Radiator. "A true fat man would never work this hard."

"Damn right," roars Hardware. "Why stand in the rain golfing when there's a clubhouse a thousand yards away with a TV and a free all-you-can-eat buffet?"

Laugeni empties a bag of M&M's into his mouth and says: "You ready to get that pie at Pepe's?"

"Hell no," says Hardy. "Let's head for the free buffet. Free is a major component of fat."

LLAMA NATION

MOUNT GREYLOCK, VERMONT

My brightest llama, Ogar, parades around the basement with an aristocratically long neck and a sophisticated droop to his eyelids. The parade usually ends when Ogar judiciously folds his front legs under him like a lawn chair and sinks into a heavily furred heap. In llama circles, such sit-ins are known as "kushing." Ogar's diffident half brother, Edgar, is not nearly so sociable. Edgar just pokes his head in the basement, hoists his haughty nose higher, and ducks out.

Ogar and Edgar are the sort of bourgeois llamas my corn-farming neighbors dismissively call "field potatoes."

A typical entry from Edgar's diary:

6 a.m. - 7a.m.: Wake up. Eat hay.

7 a.m. - 9 a.m.: Chew cud.
9 a.m. - 11 a.m.: Stand in front of electric fan.
11 a.m. - 11:15 a.m.: Nose rooster around barnyard.
11:15 a.m. - 1 p.m.: Take nap.
1 p.m. - 4 p.m.: Stand in front of electric fan.
4 p.m. - 4:15 p.m: Nose hen around barnyard.
4:15 p.m. - 6 p.m.: Take another nap.
6 p.m. - 7 p.m.: Eat more hay.
7 p.m. - 9 p.m.: Chew more cud.
9 p.m. - 10 p.m.: Free play.

The innate laziness of my llamas makes me think they'd never cut it as pack animals. Lars Garrison thinks otherwise. "They'd make great caddies," he tells me. "They have the perfect temperament. They're quiet, non-judgmental, and never argue—quite unlike many humans I've seen." While he concedes Ogar and Edgar might be a bit weak on club selection, he says: "At least you wouldn't have to tip them."

Garrison is the Dalai Lama of llama caddying, a Vermont visionary who has turned his hillside farm into the world's only llama caddying school. "The place looks like Noah's ark," says Bob Levy, whose Talamore Country Club in Southern Pines, N.C., employs six of Garrison's graduates. "And Lars is Noah."

Perched on 100 acres of wooded, alpine meadow in the shadow of Mount Greylock, West Mountain Farm serves as boot camp for 90 or so camelid caddies. Garrison's home sits dead center. "My average gelding caddy sells for $800," he says. "Usually I ask $750, but being a caddy ought to increase a llama's value." Lowball him, and all you'll get is a woolly lawn mower.

A bluff, fiercely bearded ex-oilman who wears wool shirts in deep pine-forest colors, Garrison bought the farm when he retired, in 1985. He tried harvesting apples and blueberries but soon discovered man cannot live by fruit alone. He and his wife, Gayle, considered and dismissed beef, hogs, and lambs. Then someone suggested llamas. "I did a lot of reading on them," Garrison recalls. "For instance, I learned that the Incas began domesticating them for packing nearly 3,000 years ago."

For the record, no Incan llama ever carried Calloways up an Andean slope. Llamas were considered gifts of the gods, and their ownership was restricted to royalty. Therefore, unfortunately, they made excellent sacrificial offerings. The Incas not only stuffed their llamas as beasts of burden, they stuffed themselves with their llamas. On the grand days of solar sacrifices, high priests killed a specially selected young black llama to examine his entrails for auguries. The llama's heart and lungs were removed, and his head was pointed east. If the signs were not favorable, the priests tried again with an adult male and, if that didn't work, a barren female. Tens of thousands of llamas were then decapitated, their hearts offered up to the sun, their internal organs charred as burnt offerings. The heads were turned into soup; the hides, sandals. The wool was woven into ponchos and braided into rope. Even the dung, dried, became what is facetiously called *carbon peruano*—

a fuel for *altiplano* campfires. That's more than twice the known uses for PGA caddies.

Lured by the lore of llamas, Garrison bought a pair. The herd prospered, and a few years later, Garrison read a pamphlet on how to train llamas to caddy. "The pamphlet noted how the llama's quiet nature fit right in with the atmosphere of golf courses," he says. "Their soft, padded feet rarely leave a mark, and mature, well-conditioned males can easily carry two 30-pound bags of clubs." Garrison selected two mature males and conditioned them. In 1991, he dispatched his first graduates to Talamore.

Alas, Talamore's llamas no longer caddy. The new club pro "retired" them last summer, and now they're just part of the gallery. "To employ llamas, you really need a pro-llama pro," says Bruce Brage, a Minnesota mailman whose Elmdale Hills course in Meisville is one of only a handful in the world with a llama option. "We allow ours to caddy on Mondays and Tuesdays." Before hiring his llamas, in 1995, Brage called Garrison for pointers. Today, for $40 a bag, your foursome can rent a couple of 9-year-olds named Hank and Pueblo. Toting two sets of clubs and the obligatory cooler, they'll walk the 18 holes, pausing in the rough for an occasional graze and scat stop. "Pueblo is a bit of a flincher, but he and Hank are usually well-behaved," Brage reports. "We only have trouble when a golfer lets go of the lead ropes, and the llamas trot back to their pasture next to the clubhouse. It's fun to watch the golfers come running up behind them, laughing. You can't be a serious golfer if you use a llama."

On this sun-cured Vermont afternoon, Garrison scampers for the barn to find a new pupil. Rusting by the door is an ancient New York City subway sign that reads:

Spitting on Sidewalks Prohibited
Penalty $5 to $100
Dept. of Health

"That's llama humor," Garrison says. "One of the first questions I always get is, 'Do they spit?' I always say, 'Yes, but at each other, not people.' And the people I explain this to seem to understand. It's amazing—people are educable."

Garrison surveys the dozen llamas in the barn and chooses Royal Dalton, a 6-year-old gelding with thick, rippling fur the color of nutmeg. Garrison slips a scarlet halter over the animal's head and clips on an eight-foot lead rope. "It's important to speak soothingly to potential llama caddies," Garrison says. "Isn't that right, Royal Dalton?"

"*Orgle, orgle,*" says Royal Dalton. "*Orgle, orgle, orgle.*"

"He's singing," says Garrison.

Singing what?

" 'I wanna go play golf.' "

Links llamas express themselves with an assortment of odd little tunes. They convey distress (say, after an errant tee shot lands in a pond) with a series of short, high, bike-hornlike bleats. The loud, throaty yodel they make to show fear (say, after a shot is shanked into a bear cave) suggests a very old car trying to start and failing. When content (say, after a hole-in-one), llamas emit a soft, tinkling hum that sounds like an entire orchestra of air conditioners. "The only reason they hum," cracks Garrison, "is that they don't know the words."

Garrison does. He says them in low, gentle tones while escorting Royal Dalton to a clearing in the apple orchard. He says them in even lower, gentler tones while lifting a sawbuck saddle onto the llama's back. The saddle has been specially designed to allow golf bags to be strapped over the crossbars. Royal Dalton, who has never worn one before, fixes Garrison with an archly disapproving stare. Garrison ignores him. The llama ruminates on a mouthful of clover, and kushes.

"Mind your manners, you big goat!" says Garrison.

After a few minutes of prodding and cajoling, he finally yanks the balky llama to its feet. "Are you ready to behave?" asks Garrison slowly but firmly.

Royal Dalton's head and neck shoot forward, like a chicken's. "*Orgle*," he says. "*Orgle, orgle*."

Garrison strokes him tenderly on the lower neck: "The first time I tried to teach a llama to caddy, I had golf clubs in the apple trees. It wasn't the llama's fault, it was mine."

The Lars Garrison Technique of Llama Caddying has three stages. "In Stage 1, the llama is afraid of the clubs," he says. "In Stage 2, he finds them an annoyance. By the final stage, the clubs are just something to ignore."

Royal Dalton is a quintessential Stage 1 llama. Garrison begins his first lesson by placing two empty golf bags on the ground and walking his pupil around them. Then he loads one of the bags with clubs, lets the llama sniff it, and hangs the bag from the saddle. The heads of the clubs tilt toward the llama's rump. "A llama doesn't know these are golf clubs," Garrison says. "He thinks they're noisy, rattly things that are going to jump up and bite him."

Suddenly, Royal Dalton gets spooked. He bucks wildly, scattering clubs into the apple trees. Garrison collects the woods, irons, and putters and shoves them into the bags. He strokes the llama and praises him. "Are you ready to behave?" Garrison asks at last.

"Orgle, orgle."

Garrison sets both bags against his truck. He fills a small bowl with grain, sets it between the bags, and walks away. Royal Dalton moves tentatively toward the grain and begins to eat.

"Good boy!" says Garrison, laying the clubs over the re-filled bowl. Eyes ever alert, banana ears erect, Royal Dalton enters Stage 2 by nosing through the annoying clubs to the grain. "To teach a llama, you have to see things from his perspective," observes Garrison. "Royal Dalton has decided these aren't meat-eating bags after all."

Feed finished, Garrison fills the bowl again and sets the bags beside it. Royal Dalton edges closer. Clomping his left front foot on Garrison's right, he leans down and eats. Garrison doesn't move. "That may have looked like an accident, but it was as deliberate as hell," Garrison says. "He wanted me to take a step and fall on my ass."

Garrison gets more grain. Royal Dalton clatters behind him, nuzzling lightly. This time, Garrison conceals the bowl *under* the bags. "I'm giving you more food," Garrison tells the llama, "but you'll have to go find it." Royal Dalton goes and finds it.

The llamameister tethers the llama to his pick-up and massages his shoulder with a putter.

"*Orgle, orgle*," Royal Dalton says placidly.

Garrison slides the club into a golf bag, which he props against the llama's left flank. He adds 13 more clubs, one at a time.

"*Orgle, orgle.*"

Garrison props the bag against the llama's right flank and pulls out each club, one at a time.

"*Orgle, orgle.*"

Garrison hooks the bags to the saddle and loads them with clubs.

"*Orgle!*"

He leads Royal Dalton through the trees, down hills, over loose scree. The bags bump and rattle, but the llama stays serene.

Stage 3!

"See that?" says Garrison. "Royal Dalton just taught himself to accept the fact that golf bags are okay. There isn't a single lion or tiger in them."

The session—the first of four—lasts 15 minutes. "All this training has to be reinforced three, ten, a hundred times," says Garrison. "And the hundred-and-first time, the four-legged caddy invariably steps on a wasp nest and sends clubs flying all over hell." He pauses a moment before adding: "But then, so would a two-legged caddy."

Maybe Ogar can be more than a field potato after all.

CADDYSHACKLED

HUDSON VALLEY, NEW YORK

A sk most people what they think of when they see Bill Murray, and they mention the way he mixes sarcasm with smarm. They mention the cocky *Saturday Night Live* lounge singer ad-libbing lyrics to movie themes ("*Star Wars*, nothing but *Star Wars*, gimme those *Star Wars*, don't let 'em *ennnnd!*"); or the wiseass buck private in *Stripes* pleading with the girlfriend who's leaving him ("You can't go. All the plants are gonna die"); or the smugly repellant *Groundhog Day* weatherman stuck in the groove on time's revolving record.

They mention Murray's voice, dripping with deadpan derision. They mention his lumpy yet agile body, which at charity tee-offs from Pebble Beach to the Caddyshack Invitational in St. Augustine, Florida, is often covered, like a piece of overstuffed Victorian upholstery, in outrageously garish golfing garb. But mainly they mention his face, the anonymous mug of the doctor he nearly became, puffy and pouchy and pockmarked. Oscar Wilde once said, "Intellect destroys the harmony in any face," but not even Murray could be that smart.

Murray is cruising 60—and his face looks it. His thick, graying brows convey a watchful quality that always keeps its distance. His thin, pale lips—set in a permanent smirk—register annoyance as precisely as a Geiger counter. But it's his eyes—private, withdrawn, full of self-mocking knowingness—that make his face so improbably poignant. A sudden flicker can suggest depths of disappointment or convey a kind of wry, wounded dignity.

Over a boisterous and amazingly durable career that has spanned four decades and 40 films, the onetime *Saturday Night Live* sketch comedian has subtly mutated into perhaps the greatest comic actor of his generation. "Bill's comic charisma comes from his swaggering indifference," says fellow *SNL* alumnus Mike Myers. "I see him on-screen and want to hang out with him in the worst possible way."

Not since Jack Benny has an entertainer gotten so many laughs with so little apparent effort. "There are comics who have to work very hard to get out there, to dominate a live audience, to get laughs—in short, to do comedy, which is *hard*," offers film historian David Thomson. "Alas, the hardness may enter into them, preventing the tenderness—or the pretense of tenderness—that is essential to acting." Murray is the only knight of the *SNL* round table who has broken out of his comic armor.

Lately he has all but abandoned comedy for darker terrain. Sure, he still has antic moments, but they seem to come less and less frequently. Maybe it's because, like many so-called comic geniuses—Woody Allen, Robin Williams, Steve Martin—he feels he must do serious, weighty work. Or maybe he's more interested in creating intensely real characters who are funny precisely because they are so acutely observed. Or maybe he's just an adventurous actor who likes a good challenge. "When a comedian tries to do more significant things, very often he strikes out," says Allen, who has himself whiffed in pointless paeans to foreign masters. "The urge to do more is healthy. In comedy, the quickest way to death as an artist is to repeat a successful formula over and over." Not repeating a formula, Allen adds, "is a slower way to death."

Murray's misanthropic millionaire in *Rushmore*—he famously cannonballed into a leaf-clogged swimming pool, huddled underwater, and, one imagined, wondered why he should come up at all—was hailed as a career-defining performance. He was equally magnetic in smaller roles: the drunken ventriloquist in *Cradle Will Rock* and an unctuous Polonius in *Hamlet*. In 2004, he nearly snagged an Oscar for another autumnal figure: the brittle Hollywood has-been in *Lost in Translation* who forms a hesitant bond with a young American woman staying at his Tokyo hotel. What's most haunting about Murray in *Rushmore*, is not his melancholy clowning, but the aching sadness with which he informs a Roxy Music song. Indeed, so spot-on was his performance as a put-upon character whom everyone wants a piece of, that we leave the film asking, Were we watching Murray play a role, or the real-life struggle of Murray himself?

In the 2004 film *The Life Aquatic With Steve Zissou*, Murray played an oceanographer struggling to complete his latest underwater-exploration documentary. Once again, his rich vein of ennui was mined by an adoring young director (*Rushmore's* Wes Anderson) who'd teethed on Murray's work. And once again, he was a cold fish fluffing his middle-aged gills. The middle age he depicted was bathetic, not pathetic, as it might have been in the hands of a more ingratiating comedian like, say, Robin Williams. "This is one of those rare roles that's worthy of Bill's talent," says one friend and co-star. "Usually, even when he's offered one, he turns it down." Among the better ones Murray has rejected: the lead in the first *Batman* and the autistic savant in *Rain Man*. "As choosy as Bill is," says the friend, "he's not *that* choosy."

What, if anything, could explain Murray's recent turn as the voice of the animated feline in *Garfield*? At one point—admittedly, the lowest point—he belts out "New Dog State of Mind," an alleged Billy Joel parody as painful to the ears as a kitten clawing up a chalkboard. Then again, Murray has five kids to put through college.

MANY ACTORS SAY THEY HATE THE LIMELIGHT, THEN promptly glow in it. Murray isn't one of them. He's a deeply elusive creature. *Lost in Translation* director Sofia Coppola spent five months leaving messages on his answering machine. "Stalking Bill became my life's work," she has recalled.

Even after signing on for a film, Murray has a habit of jumping ship just before shooting is about to begin. Among the extras on the *Lost in Translation* DVD is a video diary in which Coppola tells the camera, on the first day on location in Tokyo, that this is the day Murray is due to arrive and that she hopes he will. She couldn't be sure until he actually showed up.

Murray is no less inaccessible to the media. He grants as few audiences as possible. I am not heartened when a Hollywood publicist e-mails me: "Bill makes himself available for very little publicity. We are happy to pass your request along, but an interview seems highly unlikely."

While being lateralled from flack to agent to flack, I ring up Mike Veeck, the minor league baseball impresario who owns eight teams with Murray and seven other lunatics. Murray is officially the consortium's director of fun, a title bestowed on him by Veeck, who is director of titles. Veeck tells me the story of how Murray made a rain delay in Brockton, Massachusetts, endurable by leading a high school marching band in a rendition of "Mustang Sally." He tells me how, in Charleston, South Carolina, Murray hung with fans for hours, "signing everything that wasn't nailed down." He tells me how Murray packed the stadium in St. Paul with his Silent Night promotion: For the first five innings no one was allowed to make a sound. "Bill is beloved in the bushes," he says. "He's accessible to everyone." Well, not everyone.

I ask about Murray's habit of getting up people's noses. In Hollywood, he's known for being chilly, brattish, and often, insufferable. I remind Veeck of Murray's slap-down with Lucy Liu on the set of *Charlie's Angels* and his hissy fit at the 2004 Oscars—he tried to walk out after he didn't win. I bring up Murray's habit of cutting total strangers to slag to score comedic points. I mention how he seems to resent sharing the spotlight with comic George Lopez at Pebble Beach. Lopez is even more outgoing and interactive with the gallery than Murray, and he has become the tournament's dominant celebrity. "Bill has given George the cold shoulder," says a mutual friend. "George was miffed at first, but now his attitude is simply, screw Bill Murray."

Veeck insists Murray is reasonable and sane, a thoroughly decent guy. "Bill has an uncanny ability to relate to and speak to children," he says. "He respects kids and doesn't attempt to talk down to them." Golf, says Veeck, bares him—just as Buddhism bared the seeker Murray played in *The Razor's Edge*. To Murray, he says, golf is a cagey game of disappointment and intermittent reward. "Bill sees it as an experience rather than a result," offers Veeck. "He loves bucking and welcomes its mystery and rolls."

He suggests I call Van Schley, the partner perhaps closest to Murray. I do. Schley calls Murray and graciously relays my request for a powwow. "Oh, okay," Murray tells him.

I ask Schley: "And that was it?"
Schley says: "That was it."

JOHN CLEESE PROPOSES THE THEORY THAT EVERY comedian's comic character is based on the person he would have become if he'd lacked a sense of humor. In the case of Murray, this means, generally, a raspy, obnoxious, high-spirited contrarian—not unlike the Jazz Age hippie he played in the justly mauled remake of *The Razor's Edge*, which was based on the novel by Somerset Maugham. In his first dramatic role, Murray played Larry Darrell, a rich Illinois boy disgusted by the crass material-ism around him. He drops out and goes to Paris to live among the poor and ultimately heads for India to find Truth and the Meaning of Life. Both make cameos in the cloud-borne monastery at which Murray sits and beams as the soundtrack swells. Who needs enlightenment? Mur-ray's sly sneer makes him look like he's stumbled upon the world's greatest Walkman.

Growing up in a comfortable Chicago suburb, young Bill was a kind of seeker too. The fifth of nine kids (six of them boys), he constantly sought the approval of his father, Ed, a lumber salesman. To win it, he worked the dinner table. One of his most vivid childhood memories is of falling off the table while doing a Jimmy Cagney impres-sion. "I hit my head very hard on the metal foot of the table leg, and it hurt terribly," he recalled in his book, *Cinderella Story: My Life in Golf*. "But when I saw my father laugh-ing, I laughed while crying at the same time." Murray-ologists speculate that he may suffer from the western hemisphere's worst case of middle-child syndrome.

He was a class clown who got defrocked as an altar boy and kicked out of the Boy Scouts before he'd even gotten a uniform. To pay his tuition to an all-boys Jesuit school, Murray worked as a caddy. According to *Cinderella Story*, he got busted for giving a blind duffer three hole-in-one trophies. The caddy shack, he writes, taught him "how to smoke, curse, play cards. But more important, when to." He later distilled those lessons into Carl Spackler, the palsied, gopher-killing greenkeeper he invented for *Caddyshack*. Spackler, you'll recall, grows grass that "you can play 36 holes on in the afternoon, take home, and get stoned to the bejesus on at night."

In high school, Murray acted in *The Music Man* (he wanted to dance with girls), but in his words, he mostly "screwed off." He enrolled at Regis College in Denver with the idea of going into premed but screwed off some more and left school after his freshman year. In 1971, the 20-year-old dropout was busted at a Chicago airport after joking that he had bombs in his luggage. What he had was eight-and-a-half pounds of marijuana, an indiscretion for which the world's dopiest doper was placed on probation.

Suddenly, comedy didn't look so bad. In 1974, he followed his older brother Brian into Chicago's Second City improv group, which based its comedy on surprise and recognition derived from internal conflict and complex personal relationships. Murray's constant grade-school

razzing of Gilda Radner gave birth to The Nerds, who boo-
gied and noogied to Prom Night fame:

> Murray, giving Radner a noogie: "Noogie patrol!
> Here's those special prom noogies that you
> ordered. You sent away for those didn't ya?"
> Radner: "Cut it out 'Pizza Face!' You're messing up
> my hair! Boy, are you ever immature!"
> Murray, checking out her blouse: "Gee, are there
> any new developments?"
> Radner, slapping his hand: "Stop!"
> Murray: "Guess not … You know, you really oughta
> put some Band-Aids on those mosquito bites you
> got there."
> Radner: "Oh, that's so funny I forgot to laugh."

A year later, in 1975, Radner, John Belushi, and Dan
Aykroyd were recruited by Lorne Michaels for a new sketch
comedy show he was creating. Unfortunately, NBC brass
deemed Murray unready for the Not Ready for Prime Time
Players. It wasn't until the second season, after top banana
Chevy Chase bowed out, that Murray got his shot.

The cast of *SNL* was brutally competitive. To Murray's
chagrin, it took a while to crack the starting lineup; only
Aykroyd would write him into skits, and then mostly as the
second cop, with no lines. But his Lounge Singer begat Todd
the Nerd who begat the TV movie critic running down (literally) lists of Oscar nominees. Murray stuck around for
three seasons, keeping many (very many) leaden 90-minute

shows afloat with his fire and feverishness. He'd yank laughs out of lousy material, and the audience.

He parlayed his fame into a stream of broadly comic roles in eyesores like *Meatballs* and *Where the Buffalo Roam*. He stole scenes as Dustin Hoffman's roomie in *Tootsie* and hit pay dirt with *Ghostbusters*, which raked in $239 million, then the most ever for a comedy. "Bill was the nasty Jimmy Stewart," says *Groundhog Day* director Harold Ramis, and indeed, Murray's assertive obliviousness became the emblem of both outsider hipsters and insider wannabes. Not everyone was amused. Of the snarky soldier Murray portrayed in *Stripes*, critic Pauline Kael wrote: "I wouldn't want to be within 50 yards of anything he believed in."

Then, at the height of Murray's popularity, something not so funny happened. *The Razor's Edge* quietly sank into oblivion. Murray, who had co-written the script, had strong-armed Paramount into bankrolling the project on the condition that he first make *Ghostbusters*. *Razor's Edge* had been hugely important to Murray, who was hugely disappointed when it flopped. He retreated to Paris à la Larry Darrell and studied philosophy at the Sorbonne. (Unlike Larry, Bill took no vow of poverty.)

One day, he went to the Cinémathèque Française to see D.W. Griffith's 1919 film, *A Romance of Happy Valley*. "This movie just destroyed me," Murray said in 1988, when he ended his self-imposed four-year exile from Hollywood. "And I thought, How the hell can you go make *The Love Bug* if you've seen *this*?" Since then he has made good moves, bad moves, and wrong moves, but never obvious moves.

Well, except maybe *Ghostbusters II*.

I've been trying to land Murray for a solid month, and I'm still getting stonewalled. His "people" don't say yes, and they don't say no. In fact, they don't say much of anything. I commiserate with Rick Reilly, the author of *Who's Your Caddy?: Looping for the Great, Near Great, and Reprobates of Golf*. Reilly had tried to persuade Murray to let him lug his clubs for a chapter in the book. He pestered Murray's people for a year. No luck. Then, one day, for no apparent reason, Murray phoned him. He was driving on a highway near his home in New York's Hudson River Valley.

Reilly remembers saying, "How about you let me loop for you, and I'll do a chapter on it in the book?"

Murray said, "Nahhh, I don't think so."

"Ahhh, it'd be great!"

"You don't need me. You've probably got all kinds of yeses."

"No, I've got all kinds of nos."

"Who's said no to you?"

"O.J. Simpson."

Murray started giggling. And cackling. And roaring. When he finally caught his breath, he said, "You're telling me O.J. Simpson, a guy with absolutely nothing to do *but* play golf, told you no?"

Reilly: "Yep."

Murray: "What time is it?"

Reilly: "Eleven-fifteen. Why?"

Murray: "Because that's the funniest damn thing I'm gonna hear all day."

Then he hung up.

SO IS MURRAY A COMIC GENIUS, A FIGURE WHO deserves to be mentioned in the same breath as history's greats? Mike Myers says yes, conferring on him a place in Movieland Parnassus alongside Jack Benny, Bob Hope, and John Cleese. Cleese himself won't go so far. To be a comic genius in film, he says, you must have total creative control over your work. It's not enough to act in the vehicle; you must write, direct, and produce it as well, which Murray doesn't. The only living candidate he can think of is Woody Allen.

For his part, Allen calls Murray "extraordinarily skillful," but not genius material. "Lots of very talented comedians can make you laugh," he says, "but if you think of Mozart and Picasso and Shakespeare and Rembrandt, it's very difficult to find a comedian who rises to the level of genius." By Allen's count, there have been only six in the entire history of cinema, and the last one (Peter Sellers) died in 1980. The rest are Charlie Chaplin, Buster Keaton, W.C. Fields, and Groucho and Harpo Marx.

Yet film critic David Edelstein finds genius in the "hipster-clown's triumph over vulnerability," Murray's MO. "The problem for him as a 'straight' actor is how to stay true to that side of his personality," Edelstein has argued, "and yet somehow bare his soul, as a real actor must."

Misery clings to Murray like a monkey on a racehorse, and still he wins us over with the sincerity of his world-weary insincerity.

FINALLY, AFTER SIX WEEKS, AND DESPITE VAN SCHLEY'S promise, I get the definitive e-mail: "Bill Murray is a quiet person who does precious little press. Mr. Murray is not going to be available." I track down Roy Blount, whom Murray enlisted to rewrite the screenplay of *Larger Than Life*.

"A career in comedy is a tricky thing to sustain, to keep believing in, to stay loose enough for, over a lifetime," says Blount. "Just about anybody I can think of, except P.G. Wodehouse and Henny Youngman, has subsided into semi-earnestness eventually. Either they flame out, like Richard Pryor, or get ground down, like Keaton, or turn soppy, like Chaplin, or get to where they're mechanically cranking things out, like Woody Allen."

Murray, he says, is extremely slippery about picking his spots, about choosing vehicles that bring out his juices. "In part, this is self-preservation," Blount reckons, "but I also think he has a sense of mission, of keeping a certain spirit alive in the world. He's managed to work the system by being hard to pin down. He's too independent to be called an actor, exactly. He's a wonder."

Blount doesn't think he'll rent *Garfield*, though.

COCKADOODLE DOO

PORTSMOUTH, NEW HAMPSHIRE

rom the observation deck of the Perdue-AgriRecycle Pellet Plant, the towering heaps of chicken manure below look like the mountains of Mars. Thousands of tons of manure spread out in undulating drifts across the floor of the world's biggest craphouse, so huge it can fit 10 railcars at once. Unprocessed ordure is on the left; processed, on the right. Dividing these two piles of poop is a massive–for lack of a better term–"Kakatron" that looks like an exhibit left over from a science fair at Brobdingnagia High.

Choking a coffee mug that bears a picture of an anxious hen on a toilet above the caption "When you go, go with the best," plant manager Tom Ferguson guides you through the bowels of the facility, where signs say things like "Pneumatic

Dust Control." "Other companies turn out more poultry, but Perdue is the leader in turning poultry manure into money," he says. "We're No. 1 in the No. 2 business."

Every year, up to a billion pounds of raw chicken litter from Perdue farmers in Delaware, Maryland, and Virginia passes through the Kakatron like a tamale through a *turista Norteamericano*. "The litter is a blend of manure and sawmill residue," says Ferguson, sounding a bit like a proud chef in a four-star restaurant. "Our screening operation removes all the human-made debris from the mix—the misplaced wrenches, the dropped hammer handles, the lost Timex watches."

The filtered waste is baked into granules the size, shape, and texture of Post Grape Nuts. "In our own way," Ferguson says, "we're turning chicken shit into chicken salad." A conveyor system loads the delicacy onto dump trucks and railroad cars, which ship it to distributors who package it as organic fertilizer for farms, garden centers, and yes, golf courses.

Of the half-dozen companies that dole out Perdue dung to golf courses, the most evocatively named is Cockadoodle Doo. "We encourage course superintendents to *doo* the right thing," says John Packard, president of Pure Barnyard, the Portsmouth, New Hampshire outfit that markets the product. "New England has 587 18-hole courses. We have supplied chicken crap to about 20 percent of them."

That may sound like just a dropping in the bucket, but Cockadoodle only began targeting golf courses in 2004. And it's already the region's doo-doo king. "The courses here spend roughly $15 million a year on fertilizer," Packard says. "We're trying to change the marketplace one chicken at a time."

In a sense, course superintendents are farmers who grow a crop an eighth of an inch high that they never harvest. Mowing robs the crop of vital nutrients and checks root development, which can mean that water percolates too quickly through the ground and dissolves lime from the soil. It can also rob greenskeepers of their livelihood. "A lot of country club members want to play only on links that are emerald green," says Cockadoodle Doo salesman Dan O'Neill. If a patch on the 14th fairway turns to thatch, the superintendent may soon be out on the street.

Over the last half-century, most magnificent course turf has owed its perfection to industrial chemicals. Superintendents routinely doused their sod with herbicides, pesticides, fungicides, and synthetic fertilizers. "You'd see little white flags on the fairways that warned 'Stay off until dry' and would start wondering how safe it was for their children and pets," O'Neill says. "If you lived near a course and wanted to own an old dog, it helped if it was a tall dog."

To conservationists, of course, the idea of spraying grass with toxic compounds is heresy. Artificial additives can leech into water supplies. Evidently, they can also leech into greenskeepers. A 1994 University of Iowa study of superintendents with lengthy exposure to herbicides showed a 23% increase in non-Hodgkin's lymphoma, a 29% increase in prostate cancer, a 17% increase in cancer of the large intestine, and a 20% increase in brain and nervous system cancers. Not surprisingly, many superintendents have abandoned chemicals for chicken manure, which Ferguson claims "is so safe that at the end of the day, you almost want to eat it."

O'Neill demurs: "I bet it tastes like crap."

On a dull, damp autumn afternoon, O'Neill walked the 11th fairway at Turner Hill Country Club in Ipswich, Massachusetts. The ground squelched wetly underfoot. "It takes about 18 months to wean a course off chemicals," he says. "It's like heroin addiction: You've got to slowly flush the poisons out of a system." At Turner Hill, chicken manure has been embraced by John Sadowski, the 26-year-old superintendent. "The new generation of superintendents tends to be more environmentally conscious," offers Ferguson. "Some of them are organically minded, and some are such purists that they ought to wear hemp shirts and become vegans."

Sadowski is practically an organic fanatic. "Chicken crap just blows away synthetic fertilizers," he says. "It promotes bacteria, adds bulk to thin soil, and provides beneficial minerals not found in chemical additives."

Just as pro golfers monitor their diets to the nth degree, a good nutritional balance in golf course soil is critical. "Chickens are not very efficient at digesting food, and don't retain many nutrients," says Ian Grant, the CEO of Pure Barnyard. "Most of what goes in comes back out."

At Turner Hill, Sadowski applies rich dressings of nature's chocolate pudding—90 tons a year. He alternates Cockadoodle Doo's pasteurized poop with the composted crap put out by Pearl Valley Organix of Pearl City, Illinois. The latter has shot through the tailpipes of egg-layers—as opposed to Perdue's broilers—and has three times the calcium. "There's a lot of competition in this business," says Pearl Valley operations manager Andy Thompson. "My manure pretty much speaks for itself."

It also stinks for itself. The big drawback with chicken manure is the smell—which can be diabolical. "In the fertilizer world," allows Ferguson, "everything's got an odor." But not one that repels Essex County Club superintendent Pat Kriksceonaitis, a Cockadoodle Doo diehard. "I think chicken manure has a sweet aroma," he says. "To me, it's a real positive."

That can quickly change if, during the dog days of summer, a golfer sticks his fertilizer-caked shoes in the trunk of his car and forgets about them for a few weeks. "Things could get a little ugly," Kriksceonaitis concedes, "but that's the price you pay for playing golf on chicken manure."

Animal waste is available to courses in an almost infinite number of varieties. Fertilizers feature everything from sheep scree (commonly called Ba-Ba Doo) to cow patties (Moo Doo). At its semiannual "Fecal Fests," the zoo in Woodland Park, Washington, sells Zoo Doo, a shotgun wedding of bedding straw and elephant, hippo, zebra, giraffe, gazelle, and oryx manure.

The North Shore Country Club in Mequon, Wisconsin, douses its T-boxes with Father Don's Duck's Doo Compost, food for the soil *and* soul that includes duck manure, cranberries, rice hulls, wood shavings, vanilla beans, and pickles. Founded by a Roman Catholic priest from Kenosha, the nonprofit outfit uses the slogan "Complete the Loop—Buy Duck Poop!"

But when it comes to wretched excess, nothing in the golfing universe trumps You Doo, the euphemism for the human excrement processed by Synagro in Texas. During the winter months, it's used to melt ice on courses as much as it is to fertilize them.

Selling sewage sludge to country clubs may sound like the crappiest job in golf, but at least Synagro staffers have a sense of humor about it. Employees joke that when they go on bathroom breaks, they're just simply adding to the company's bottom line.

GOLF BUFFS

CYPRESS GROVE, FLORIDA

Warm and friendly and thoroughly tanned, Ray Peterson is the kind of guy who would give you the shirt off his back. Assuming he had a shirt on his back. On this particular March afternoon, he doesn't. Striding down the fairways at the Cypress Cove golf course, the 56-year-old mechanical engineer looks perfectly at ease wearing nothing more than a cowboy hat and the broadest of grins. "I always play without shoes," he says. "I don't feel comfortable in them."

Or anything else.

Peterson is one of 30 male and female naturists, aged 37 to 76, teeing it up in Central Florida during the sport's quintessential skins game. "The human body is not meant to be in a bra and underwear," says Sandi Tayler, whose own body isn't in either. Showing not a trace of embarrassment, with unclothed parts flapping free, she and her fellow duffers give proof that every action has an equal and opposite reaction.

The nine-hole pitch-and-putt course takes up two and a half acres of the Cypress Cove Nudist Resort & Spa, a veritable Garden of Eden of saunas, swimming pools, tennis courts, hot tubs, and spring-fed lakes. Of the 272 nudist clubs in the United States and Canada, it's one of only two with its own links. "Too bad the pros won't strip down like us—most are too staid and straitlaced," allows Tayler's husband, John, 56. "I'd like to see John Daly go naked, though." The rest of us would likely avert our gaze.

With its silly check trousers and paunchy polo shirts, golf may be the most sartorially ludicrous of all sports. But playing in your birthday suit? "Actually," deadpans Sam Jackson, the president of the Cypress Cove Golf Association, "my golf outfit is transparent."

The 66-year-old ex-Marine believes golf is enhanced without attire. He likes the feeling of the sun on his belly and the breeze against his butt. He likes the sense of lightness, of being totally unencumbered. "Normally, after a day out on the greens I'd come back with a golfer's tan," he says. "Here, there are no tan lines."

To be fair, nudist golf has it disadvantages. "You've got no pockets," carps Peterson. "There's nowhere to keep your tees or balls or billfold." And after a ride on a golf cart, you may have trouble dividing your genitals from the seat. That's one reason nudists always carry towels.

Visitors would be wise not to call Cypress Cove a nudist colony. "Some members are offended by the term," says operations manager Ted Hadley. "They think it sounds like 'leper colony'." Nudist "community" is perhaps more in keeping with the intent of Hadley's late grandfather, Jim, who built the resort to provide a sanctuary for those who didn't just want to sunbathe in the altogether, but to live life *au naturel.*

Cypress Cove was unveiled during the Kennedy Administration, and four decades later it's still unabashedly going strong. "No Shirt, No Shoes, No Problem" reads the sign over the door of the administration building. Clothing is pretty much optional. The swimming area that abuts Cheeks Bar & Grill ("Rest Yours at Ours") is the only place nudism is compulsory. The rule is meant to discourage gawpers. Naturists use two sobriquets to describe clothed holidaymakers: textiles and weirdos.

Just as it is at most country clubs, Cypress Cove's 3,300 members tend to be conservative Republicans, affluent white folks looking for a safe, crime-free environment. Some are full-time residents, but for most the resort is a weekend and vacation spot. "The average age is between 40 and 50," says Jackson. "Lots members are parents who waited until their kids left the nest and then said, 'Let's do something crazy!'"

In 1993, longtime resident Mike Wax had the crazy idea to turn a wooded corner of the club into a short course. He laid out nine holes, from 25 to 48 yards. The first sand hazards were berms in the shape of nudes. One was modeled after Ivan Thomsen, Cypress Cove's general manager. "I forget what all the characteristics were," says Hadley. "But if you looked at it long enough, you could tell it was supposed to be Ivan."

Erosion has long since erased the sand sculptures. Today the biggest hazards are the stands of scrub oak. The toughest, oakiest hole is seven, which requires either a dogleg or a difficult punch shot through the tree trunks to a green bordered by clusters of skunk cabbage. Most indigenous plants are suitable for a nudist golf course. Except maybe those with prickles.

The golfers who signed up for Saturday's best-ball challenge wouldn't have cared if the grass had been sown with poison ivy. Risk-averse nudists they were not: They dined, after all, on chili, a cuisine with great potential to backfire. And despite a blazing sun, hardly any of them wore sunblock. "I haven't in 15 years," said Sandi Tayler. Which explains the Cheetos-colored rash that crept across her torso.

Here, there, and everywhere, body parts—normally concealed from public view—bobbed, swayed, and quivered. Some breasts were the size of Pinnacles; others hung like head covers stuffed with bricks. Some men had chest hair thicker than muskrat pelts; some women had hair on their heads, but nowhere else. A few of the ladies wore day dresses, untied and unbuttoned. A few of the gents wore bulging T-shirts from which drooped what looked to be a Thanksgiving turkey's giblets. No woman carried a purse, though one man sported a colostomy bag. In case you were wondering, his bag didn't match his shoes.

Jackson was as naked as his ambition. "First prize is fifteen dollars and I'm going to win it," he said before tee time. "I take this game very seriously."

Which is not that easy. When you golf in the buff, just about everything sounds suggestive. Even the phrase "watch your swing" takes on new meaning. To prep for the tournament, Jackson had played a round on Friday with a couple of guys he dubbed Bill and Big Bill. For the record, Big Bill was a full head taller.

Nudists mostly avoid risqué repartee. But pack 30 of them on a tight course and the ricocheting double entendres are inescapable.

"It's long, *real* long."
"It's not *that* long, is it?"
"Believe me, it's *long*."
"Did you stay up, Sam? Please tell me you stayed up."
"Yeah, I'm up."
"Pam, can you loosen up on your grip?"
"Stroke it a little more gently, Al."
"He jumps on Len's misses every chance he gets."
"By golly, what I wouldn't give for another three inches."
"If you'd been straight, Marv, that puppy would have gone in."

Jackson bantered best with partner Kathy Preece, a 50-year-old nudist camper who had parked her trailer home off the 1st tee. The other member of his threesome declined to divulge her last name. "You don't ask naturists a lot of questions unless they volunteer the answers," offered Jackson, a diminutive man who tries to not poke his nose into other people's business. "A lot of them want to keep their private lives private."

With Preece putting badly and Anonymous chipping madly, Jackson kept the team in contention until the back side. By the time his nude crew reached Hole 5, however, they'd gone belly up. Preece lashed her tee shot so hard that it hurtled past the cup and nearly struck a wooden wall, prompting a bystander to shout: "Hole found in nudist club fence. Police looking into it." The threesome finished with a 48, nine under par and five strokes off the lead.

Hanging out at Cypress Cove tournaments is one thing; competing in them is something else entirely. "They're fun, but they're not my bag," says Tom Grimm, who sat this one out. He prefers going the Full Monty on regulation 18-hole courses. For years, the resort had sponsored excursions to Bull Run in nearby Poinciana. Alas, Hurricane Charlie rendered Bull Run unplayable. "It's a shame," says Grimm. "You'd stand there in the nude and knock the ball as far as you could. It was grip it and rip it."

Ouch!

A VILLAGE TAKES IT

NORTH HILLS, NEW YORK

Over the past half century, Deepdale Golf Club has been swallowed up in three great controversies. The first was in 1955, just before its original course was cleaved by the Long Island Expressway and the club was moved from the village of Lake Success to neighboring North Hills. A better ball tournament with a $45,000 Calcutta pool turned into a murky mess that involved an impostor, a ringer, and phony handicaps. The shenanigans outraged USGA executive director Joseph Dey, who declared, "Consciously or unconsciously, the men who support these pools are using golf as a medium to prostitute golf."

Scandal number two unfolded that same year at the club's new home on the sprawling estate once owned by tycoon W.R. Grace. Though three of Grace's grandchildren had agreed to sell his beloved Tullaroan estate to Deepdale for $950,000, the fourth, Michael, refused to transfer his share or move out of the 40-room Georgian mansion intended for the clubhouse.

In a lawsuit, Deepdale's owners accused the young scion of trying to distract duffers with noisy tractors, speeding cars, galloping horses, unleashed dogs, women in scanty swimsuits, and actors "auditioning" for a Broadway musical. The feud ended in 1958, when Michael was evicted.

The figure at the heart of Deepdale's latest entanglement is North Hills mayor Marvin Natiss, a 23-handicapper who wants to use powers of eminent domain to turn the elite private course into an elite municipal course for dues-paying village residents. "Deepdale would be a wonderful amenity for the people of the village," he says, as if the club were a mint on a hotel-room pillow. Not that Natiss's constituency lacks links (or much of anything else: The U.S. Census Bureau has judged North Hills to be one of the wealthiest communities in the Northeast, with a per capita income of $100,093). There are 20 courses within five miles of the village and 51, including 11 public tracks, within 15 miles.

The members of Deepdale, of course, are outraged by the mayor's proposal. When he ordered environmental-impact statements and appraisals, they sued to head off a hostile takeover. "It's an undisguised land grab that would set a staggering precedent and affect every golf club in America," says Theodore Mirvis, one of the club's attorneys. "It's about stealing a golf club to increase property values in the village. It's about greed and putter-envy."

Joseph Grundfest, a law professor at Stanford and one of the leading authorities on eminent domain, views the standoff through a slightly different lens. "On one side you have the very rich," he says. "On the other, the filthy rich. It's a kind of class struggle Karl Marx never anticipated."

Neither, perhaps, had the U.S. Supreme Court. In a landmark eminent-domain ruling in June, 2005, the Supremes voted 5-4 to uphold the right of the city of New London, Connecticut, to demolish homes in an aging neighborhood to make way for an urban redevelopment zone. "The political leaders of New London were trying to address the economic distress that gripped the city after major employers had left the region," Grundfest says. "But the People's Republic of North Hills has something altogether different in mind."

Deepdale members believe that particular "something" goes against the intent of the court's decision. "To condemn a blighted property and develop it into a hospital or an orphanage—to do something for the public good—I could understand," says club member John Wilson, a retired Wall Street trader. "But the mayor is using eminent domain for private gain, not public use. The law is being perverted. There's nothing distressed in North Hills."

Snuggled on the tony Gold Coast of Long Island's North Shore, North Hills is a bedroom community of 1,800 households about 20 miles from Manhattan. Most of the 4,500 villagers live in gated enclaves; one is even called The

Enclave. North Hills has no firehouse, police department, library, or school. (If there's a blaze or a disturbance, departments from neighboring towns are summoned.) It does, however, have two golf courses. The membership of North Hills Country Club includes 60 village residents, one of whom is the deputy mayor. Deepdale, which has about 250 members, is not only more expensive (initiation: $100,000) but also more exclusive. Only one of its members—Wilson—lives in North Hills.

During its 81-year history Deepdale has counted Dwight Eisenhower, Baron Guy de Rothschild, and the Duke of Windsor as members, and more recently has had on its rolls Tiki Barber, Tom Brokaw, Sean Connery, Sidney Poitier, and New York City mayor Michael Bloomberg. "None of our members are notorious," says Wilson, who never had to fill out a foursome with the most infamous Deepdaler, Richard Nixon. "Maybe some are nefarious." Wilson adds, "Membership is by invitation only."

The idea to have the townsfolk snatch the course from the landed gentry was first floated by John Lentini, the previous mayor of North Hills. In 2002, shortly before his death, Lentini said, "We believe our acquisition of the Deepdale Golf Club will be the crown jewel of our community and bring us a new level of North Shore Gold Coast affluence."

At first Deepdalers didn't take the talk seriously. "We figured it was too preposterous," says Wilson. Then Natiss succeeded Lentini and the rhetoric started sounding like a policy statement. "As bizarre and surreal as it seemed," Wilson says, "we started to become very concerned."

Wilson is the force behind the Coalition for Deepdale, a group that has waged a large-scale public relations campaign on behalf of the club. The alliance accuses Natiss of colluding with real estate developers, a charge that Natiss denies. A condemnation, the coalition claims, would increase property taxes, not property values. "The plan to seize Deepdale is socialist!" Wilson says. "It's Communist! It's Bolshevik!" Village mailboxes brim with anti-Natiss propaganda. "Even I have been invited to join the Coalition to Bash the Mayor," says the mayor. "Obviously, I haven't joined."

The Vladimir Lenin of North Hills has been a Republican for nearly 40 years. "I wasn't looking for trouble," Natiss says. "Really, I wasn't." He's a practicing lawyer and a former town judge with a good sense of humor and a bad hip. "I don't pay attention to what I'm called by the millionaires and billionaires of Deepdale," he says defiantly. "Stick and stones may break my bones, but names will never harm me."

Natiss claims that he hasn't decided whether to invoke the principle of eminent domain. "I'm still gathering data," he says. "I've never said I would pursue this, yet the club has threatened me and backed me against the wall. I'm an elected official. I will not be scared off or intimidated."

He bristles at the notion of seizure. "This would have nothing to do with seizing property," says Natiss. "Eminent domain requires fair market value." But Deepdale's value is a subject of considerable debate. According to the club, the 175-acre property is worth more than $100 million. Natiss says county assessors recently valued Deepdale at less than $13 million. "I think [the value is] somewhere in between," he says. "However, if the actual figure turns out to be $100 million, the village couldn't afford the acquisition."

For now, the takeover has been tabled. "A condemnation may never happen," Natiss says. "Still, in my reading of the law, it would be perfectly legal. If Deepdale's members don't like the law or the evolution of the law, let them change it."

Ironically, the original Deepdale course in Lake Success was ravaged by public domain—three holes were surrendered for the Long Island Expressway—and rescued by that village's legal high jinks. In 1955, residents of Lake Success voted to purchase the club at "a fair and reasonable" price and put the parcel on the open market. The community then prevented the new buyer from subdividing the land into a housing development by rezoning the township and passing an ordinance that forbade the removal of sod from local property. Reluctantly, the builder sold Old Deepdale to the village. It's now a municipal course.

WIFFLE WHILE YOU WORK

SHELTON, CONNECTICUT

AWiffle golf ball will not dent a duck. Or a chicken. Or, for that matter, a turkey. I know this because my daughters play Wiffle golf in our barnyard. Farm rules dictate that braining a turkey with a Wiffle golf ball is a birdie. A chicken is an eagle. And a duck is a hole-in-one. We've had lots of fowl balls around the poultry pen, but so far, not one dead duck.

This property of benignity accounts for much of Wiffle golf's appeal. "Will not damage property, hurt bystanders or players," boasted the box holding the original Wiffle ball in 1954. Five decades later the box crows, "Hit It! Bounce It! Safe Anywhere!"

"However," says David A. Mullany, "in today's litigious society, one never knows." He ought to know. He's the guy for whom the Wiffle ball was invented. He even took the first whiff.

Mullany was 13 when his old man, David N., gave birth to the Wiffle baseball in Fairfield, Connecticut. Bullied off the local diamonds, the boy had to play ball in the unfriendly confines of his backyard. He and his buddies would swat at plastic golf balls with a sawed-off broomstick. "Those balls were hard to pitch," David A. recalls. "I'd snap my wrist to get rotation, and by the end of the day, my arm would be like jelly."

One night, young David A. told his father that his arm was breaking off from throwing golf ball scroogies. David N., a former semipro pitcher, was almost broke himself. His car-polish company had recently gone into bankruptcy. In need of a new career, he decided to fashion a perforated ball that would behave somewhat like the real thing.

Mullany the Elder razored designs into some plastic moldings made to hold perfume bottles. Round and hollow, the casings were slightly smaller than baseballs. Mullany the Younger tested each prototype in the backyard. Most were duds. But kitchen-table tinkering produced a ball with a solid bottom half and eight elongated holes on the top half. The ball swooped like a barn swallow and didn't strain young Mullany's arm. So old Mullany took out a second mortgage on his house and filed for U.S. patent 2,776,139: the Wiffle ball. The march of progress is irrepressible.

Calling the ball Wiffle was David A.'s idea. "You swung and missed so much," he says, "it just seemed logical." Every bit as logical as dropping the "h" in "whiffle." "I came up with that, too," says Mullany. "I told my dad it would be cheaper to make signs with fewer letters."

Wiffle Ball Inc. is a cozy little operation. David A. ascended to the presidency several years before his father's death in 1990. His two sons, David J. and Steve, are the firm's vice presidents. The family's marketing strategy is minimalist: Advertising and promotion are disdained, player endorsements taboo. "Today's athletes demand too much money," Mullany says. "We're trying to keep our balls affordable." The first Wiffle ball retailed for 49 cents; over 54 years, the same model has "inflated" to a retail price of $1.08. A Wiffle bat and ball sells online for $3.39. And a pack of six Wiffle golf balls goes for $2.25.

For more than a half-century, the Mullanys have stamped out plastic balls in a modest two-story brick building in Shelton, some 20 miles from Fairfield. An injection-molding machine coughs up Wiffle ball halves with a consumptive wheeze. Another machine seals them together. Balls—in junior, baseball, and softball sizes—roll out several at a time, every two or three seconds.

With its roundhouse curves and cutouts, the Wiffle ball has been called the most unaerodynamic projectile ever conceived. "Maybe it is," Mullany says with a shrug. "Personally, I have no idea why a Wiffle ball whiffles."

Did he and his father ever ponder its Wiffleness? "Yeah, for a couple of minutes. But what the hell's the difference?"

There's a kind of immortality in being the son of the father of the Wiffle ball. During the summer, Wiffle fans send Mullany reminiscences of legendary Wiffle golf matches, crayon diagrams of Wiffle courses, and dozens of requests for the official Wiffle rules he and his dad cooked up in the mid-1950s. "I'm happy people write in for the rules," Mullany says. "The game has a million variations."

The one played on my farm employs Great Pyrenees for flags. That's a personal concession. If I didn't let my dogs participate in Wiffle golf, they would run off with my Wiffle golf club. Mullany insists that the pooch who can re-sist Wiffle plastic has not yet been born. "If Wiffle golf ball sales ever drop," he cracks, "I'd consider flavoring them with dog food."

GOLFER IN TRAINING

LINWOOD, PENNSYLVANIA

The shiny black Hudson locomotive circling endlessly in Ed Dougherty's toy-train museum is as solid as a 10-year-old's heartbeat. Sparks sputter from under the wheels, smoke trails from the stack, and when the engine clatters past the Lionel newsstand, lanterns light up, a newsie moves forward, a paperboy spins around with his extras, and a Dalmatian jitterbugs with a fireplug. Dougherty watches this buzzing activity with the ingenuousness of a boy nearing 60. "My golf career won't last forever," he says wistfully. "But my love of trains will."

Dougherty has been chugging bravely along the tracks of the pro tours since 1975, toting up more than $2 million in prize money. In 1995, at the maddeningly precocious age of 47, he earned his lone PGA victory in the Deposit

Guaranty Classic. He also had three top-20 finishes and was tied for the lead in the Honda Open after the second round; he stayed on the leader board until flying off the rails in the fourth round. Three years later he joined the Champions circuit, and two years after that he won his first event, the Coldwell Banker Burnet Classic at Bunker Hills. The $240,000 first-place prize was more than he'd made in his best year on the PGA Tour. Dougherty recognizes what an anomaly that performance was. "Sundays are like train wrecks for me," he says. "I come into the 18th hole spewing oil. Not leaking, spewing! If not for Sundays, I'd be buying a lot more trains."

As it is, Dougherty owns nearly every choochoo made by Lionel from 1946 to 1969. His collection is housed in a converted garage behind his mother's house in Linwood, Pennsylvania. (He designed the two-story structure between rounds at the 1987 New Orleans Open.) Downstairs he keeps Western civilization's most complete assemblage of postwar Lionel poster art and advertising displays. Upstairs, shelves that reach almost to the ceiling are stacked with hundreds of trains—polished-up mementos from decades of Christmases, and survivors of thousands of high-speed derailments.

"Lionel is probably the most popular train today," says Dougherty. "It's got to be the most widely collected." He pronounces Lionel "Lie-NELL," which is how most collectors say the name of the company Joshua Lionel Cohen started at the turn of the century. Cohen started the long, long Lionel line with a 19th-century electric locomotive that was modeled after the engine the B&O Railroad used to pull trains through Baltimore's Howard Street Tunnel. "All I've got is Lie-NELL," Dougherty states. "It's the only ... " He stops abruptly, having lost his train of thought.

Dougherty got into training while still in utero. His pregnant mom bought him a freight set with a log-dump car, a coal loader, and a searchlight caboose. He still has it, as well as the Red Texas Special diesel passenger set Santa brought him when he was 7. A premature Gomez Addams, young Ed would run the freight engine west and the diesel east on the same track. "I staged fantastic crashes," Dougherty recalls. "I stopped when I realized Santa wasn't leaving me trains anymore."

One day in his 20s, Dougherty walked into a hobby shop and spied a Marx locomotive, a black, streamlined Commodore Vanderbilt Hudson type with steam domes, handrails, and the New York Central oval up front. The engine cost two bucks, the cars a quarter. He turned the cars over and saw the beer can labels on the scrap tin they'd been stamped out of. "I looked at that train and said, This is it!" Doughtery says. "I want to do this for the rest of my life."

Play with trains, of course. But his trains are hardly toys; in fact, his toys are hardly toys–they're the stuff of collections: the American Flyers of childhood, the Tootsie toys of the past, the Plastivilles of make-believe.

Dougherty began collecting trains in earnest in his 30s. He was so earnest that he painted WANTED: LIONEL TRAINS on the bottom of his golf bag and kept it like that for six years. He now routinely skips Wednesday pro-ams to poke around hobby shops and add to his collection. During the 1978 Greater Milwaukee Open, he bought out an entire train store.

He often swaps choice models to get choicer ones: "If I have to, I'll divest myself of trains." He sounds like Commodore Cornelius Vanderbilt, lopping off a couple of unprofitable lines in upstate New York. The favorite he traded up for is a Blue Comet Standard gauge 400E. "That's a big thing, 31⅜ inches from the cowcatcher to the tip of the coupler on the tender, a big Vanderbilt tender, tank-shaped. Lionel made the 400E from 1931 to 1939. The passenger cars were blue also. Those cars were 15⅓ inches long. There were three cars in a set, so it made quite a long train, about eight feet long." A majestic blue train worthy of Lionel's golden age.

Sometimes Dougherty collects and golfs simultaneously. At an event in 1992, he made a deal with a spectator on the 3rd tee. The haggling for Dougherty's prize 1957 rolling-stock Ferris wheel display took considerably longer. He'd spotted it years before in a Northampton, Massachusetts, train store, but the owner, Chip Childs, wouldn't sell it. "The only way you're going to get it," Childs told Dougherty, "is to come in first at a tournament."

Dougherty called Childs the day after he lost a sudden-death playoff at the 1990 Greater Milwaukee Open. "Hey, Chip," he said. "When am I going to get that Ferris wheel display?"

"What do you mean?" said Childs. "I said win."

"No, you said come in first," Dougherty said triumphantly, "which I did."

Dougherty hurt his shoulder in 1995 while lifting one of his 60 vintage pinball machines. "During the recuperation," he says, "hunting down old train displays was the one thing that kept me sane." That and knowing that he'd soon be eligible for the Senior tour. "It was like going from the National League to the American League," Dougherty recalls excitedly. "There were whole new towns I'd never been to and whole new golf courses I'd never played on."

Not to mention whole new train shops he had never haggled in. "My life is measured in Lionel electric trains," Dougherty says. "They were the trains my dad bought his boy." And the trains railroad men buy *their* boys.

TO HONOR THE FATHER

MASONTOWN, WEST VIRGINIA

The green hills of West Virginia rise at the steps of St. Zita Parish Church in Masontown and roll away in rounded ranks like men bent at their work in the coal pits. This is the landscape of Nick Helms' memory. These are the comfortable hills of home. Helms grew up here. He learned to play golf here. And on Jan. 2, 2006, his father, Terry, was killed in the soft coal heart of these hills.

Terry Helms was among the 13 men trapped in the Sago mining accident. During a thunderstorm, a bolt of lightning apparently struck a pocket of methane in a sealed shaft, knocking down a wall near the entrance. Terry, a fire boss, had checked for hazardous gases before the other miners were allowed inside. At age 50, he was a man of compassion and courage who was always willing to help others to the limits of his ability and his wallet. He was the first of the 12 miners to die.

It's now Jan. 10, the day of Terry's funeral, and the utility poles in Masontown are adorned with black bows and ribbons. Inside St. Zita, the Reverend Michael Bransfield, bishop of the diocese of Wheeling-Charleston, presides at the liturgy. Hundreds of mourners sit listening intently. They nod and weep and praise Terry in a ceremony full of testimony and hymn singing.

Nick watches the service from the front pew. When he learned of the cave-in, he was 560 miles away, in Myrtle Beach, South Carolina, struggling to pursue his dream of becoming a professional golfer. He drove straight home and hasn't slept much since. The priest calls him to the lectern. Looking frazzled, tired, and considerably older than his 25 years, Nick stands for a long moment in the silence of the waiting church. He smooths out a sheet of paper and speaks in a halting, breathless voice, struggling to define his father. A small muscle works in Nick's face each time he mentions Terry.

"I heard a song on the radio that reminded me of my dad," Nick says, checking his tears. "It kind of sums up how my sister, Amber, and I feel about him." Suddenly Kenny Chesney's "Who You'd Be Today" echoes through the nave of the plain brick church:

Sunny days seem to hurt the most
I wear the pain like a heavy coat

I feel you everywhere I go
I see your smile, I see your face
I hear you laughing in the rain
I still can't believe you're gone.

Less than a year before, Terry had literally kicked his only son out of West Virginia. "My dad worked 12-hour days and came home dog tired," Nick said after the funeral. "He didn't want me to be a coal miner. He pretty much forbade it. He didn't want me to bust my butt to put food on the table, like he had. He didn't want me to wear down, like he did. He wanted me to have a different life, a better life. When I took my time, he got the point across with a boot in the ass. It hurt like hell too."

Though Nick had never taken a formal golf lesson, had been saddled with a childhood disability, and hadn't played competitively since high school, Terry encouraged him to move south and give professional golf a shot. "I'd always fantasized about playing against guys I idolized," Nick says. "Dad kept telling me to go for it."

Which Nick did, settling in Myrtle Beach with his girl-friend, Kristen Sauro. He pulled his own weight, as they say in the mines, working small jobs to pay down his substantial debts and finance the $20,000 he needed for golf school. "I can make the pro tour," he says, even though he is a seven handicapper. "I have the game. I only need a little bit of help, like everybody else. The big difference between Tiger Woods and me is opportunity. He got a chance to start playing at a younger age than I did."

Helms reckons that all he needs is a year or so of instruction and six to eight hours a day on the course. "Once I get down to scratch, it'll all be course management," he says with unshakable certainty. "By the time I'm 35, I'll be pretty much set. I'm not saying I'll go out there and win the Masters the first time out, but hey, who knows?"

To those who suggest that 26 is a bit old to embark on a career in pro golf, Helms says, "Anybody who tells me it's too late—that's an ignorant opinion. They don't have my drive."

That drive, he says, comes from Terry. "Dad always said you get what you work for," Nick says. "If you don't have what you want, you didn't work hard enough for it."

Nick has had to work hard for just about everything in his life. "It's been tough for him since the very beginning," says his mother, Mary. "He was a tornado baby." Nick, who was born two months premature, was delivered in the dark during a tornado. He was placed in a neonatal unit, where for days he was tubed and suctioned. "His lungs weren't developed," Mary recalls. "The doctors didn't think he'd make it. At two weeks, Nick's heart stopped beating, and he actually died in my arms."

He was revived but not relieved. "Nick cried for a whole year," Mary says. "I thought he hated me and didn't want me as his mother." The problem turned out to be a staph infection that raged through his right side. The damage was discovered during exploratory hip surgery when Nick was a year old; he subsequently spent six months in a full body cast. "His legs were at right angles to his torso and bent at the knees," Mary says. "He looked like a goal-post." The infection left Nick's right leg an inch shorter than his left and accounts for his lopsided gait.

Born in Morgantown, Nick lived for five years in a trailer in Tunnelton, a snip of a village named for its location at the eastern end of the Baltimore & Ohio Railroad tunnel, once the longest in the world. Eventually his parents built a house in Newburg, a hardscrabble town in which people die at home with their families around them or in the mine with the mountain fallen on them. "We weren't poor, and we weren't rich," Nick says. "We had what we needed."

The Appalachian coalfields run from the West Virginia panhandle down through Kentucky, and nowhere underground is the life of a miner easy. "It's good money," says Nick, "but awful work." Terry had wanted to be a forest ranger, but he'd had a family to support. He began to harvest coal at 18 and stayed at it for 32 years. "Dad never said anything about how dangerous his job was," says Nick. "He downplayed everything."

Perhaps that explains why Nick downplays his infirmities. Hobbled and unable to raise his right arm above his head, he still played baseball and basketball, and he tried to play football. "My physical problems don't matter," he says. "Never have. You do what you have to do."

He picked up golf at 14. One day, his grandfather Francis Barlow drove him to the Paradise Lake course near Morgantown and handed him a club. "I started beatin' it and got hooked," Nick says. He practiced every day, often with his father, who was such an ardent hacker that he'd play nine holes after a long shift in the mine. "I'd practice regardless of the weather," Nick says. "Me and Dad once played in a downpour for three hours. Sleet, snow—it didn't matter if the sky was black. It just didn't matter."

In his senior year at Preston High, Helms made the taxi squad of the golf team. "It took great effort for Nick to compete, especially on courses that were hilly," says Mike Contic, the Preston coach at the time, "but he never complained. More than anything, Nick was an inspiration to the team. The other golfers had more talent but not more desire. His heart is as big as the ocean."

Helms picked up pointers and pocket change working in the bag room at three area courses. The best part was that he could play for free. "Nick's game had serious limitations," says Brad Westfall, a four-time West Virginia PGA Player of the Year, who worked at one of the clubs. "His handicap limited his swing; he couldn't hit for much distance." Even now, Helms' drives average only about 265 yards.

His golf education took a setback when he was 18. While Helms was working in a roof-bolt factory, the tip of his left index finger was crushed in a 5,000-ton housing press. "You'd be surprised how much you miss your fingertip," he says blithely. "At first it was really painful every time I swung a club, like the worst pinch you ever felt. I had to learn to deal with it."

He dealt with tuition at West Liberty State (95 miles northwest of Newburg, near the Ohio border) by driving a truck and delivering pizza. He studied golf management but didn't make the golf team. After three years, he quit school, dead broke. "I put golf on the back burner to make ends meet," he says. But the ends never met. By the time he got to Myrtle Beach, in July 2005, Helms owed $35,000. "It doesn't seem too much until you're paying it," he says.

The $285,000 he got from his father's life insurance policy and the mining company changed all that. He settled his debts, bought new cars for himself and Kristen and, on a lark, a set of 600 knives advertised on the Cutlery Corner Network. "I was flipping through the channels one night and saw a bowie knife with wolves etched into the handle," he says. "I thought, Dad would really love that. Maybe he wants me to get it." Two hundred dollars got him dozens of steak knives, butcher knives, pocket knives, hunting knives, pen knives, even a ceremonial ninja sword.

Helms also splurged on a $6,000 engagement ring. He proposed to Kristen in February before a Brad Paisley concert. Paisley, a country music star from West Virginia, had invited the families of the 13 Sago miners to be his back-stage guests. "My father said if anything happened to him, I should buy a ring and marry Kristen," Helms says. "He figured I'd never find anyone better." Nick, Kristen, and Bandit, their black Labrador puppy, share a two-story Surf-side duplex that's decorated in late Green Day.

His biggest extravagance has been the $20,000 he plunked down to enroll at the Myrtle Beach campus of the San Diego Golf Academy. Nestled in a Waccamaw Boulevard strip mall, the school offers a curriculum heavy on teaching techniques and psychology. Students earn an associate degree in applied business in 16 months and play a bunch of golf while doing it. Some graduates go on to become teachers, course managers, sales reps, or club technicians. Others wind up working in pro shops for minimum wage.

Classes began on May 1. Helms had his first lesson two days later. In his first open rounds—competitions that are part of the curriculum—he shot 90 and 92. "Nick has a long way to go if he wants to qualify for a PGA Tour card," says Brian Hughes, an academy instructor. "Of course, making the PGA Tour would be long odds for anybody. But if he has the desire and the work ethic, well ... it wouldn't shock me."

Helms' early results have prompted some reevaluation. "If I don't become a pro golfer, I'd like to teach golf," he says. "After I get my certificate from the academy, I'll have a good chance of getting a job in the industry." Until then, he'll devote much of his spare time to funding golf lessons for West Virginia schoolkids.

He has already sunk $2,000 of his inheritance into the Terry Helms Scholarship Foundation for Coal Miners' Children. He plans to bankroll the charity with donations, silent auctions, and celebrity tournaments. Miles Blundell, the head pro at Nemacolin Country Club in Farmington, Pennsylvania, helped organize an event there in 2007.

"My goal is to make my dad proud of me," Helms says. He sighs and his voice drops to a whisper. "Dad gave his life to get me to this point. Golf is what he wanted me to do, and I'll try my damnedest to find a way to do it."

THE BIRDIES AND THE BEES

SAVANNAH, GEORGIA

As pale as he is plump, aging smoothie Ed Schneider stumbles along a Savannah fairway in an advanced state of disrepair. The 54-year-old divorcé started swigging Southern Comfort on the practice green and here at the 4th hole looks permanently potted. "Hey, girls," he tells the two middle-aged women in his foursome. "Whattaya say we just get naked and jump in a pile?"

Though neither takes him up on the offer, one woman asks, "What's in the bottle?"

Schneider unscrews the fifth and passes it around. "Smells like medicine," sniffs the other woman.

"That's what I use it for," says Schneider, lubricating the idea with another mouthful. "You never know where in the rough there might be a rattlesnake. If you're bitten, whiskey will numb the poison."

The first woman looks skeptical. The second rallies. "Okay," she allows. "I'll have a sip." She takes one and says: "It's sweet!" By the 8th hole, she's taking long slugs.

"Women, booze, and golf," Schneider exults. "This is my kind of club."

Schneider's club is the American Singles Golf Association, a love n' links outfit with only two rules: You've got to bring your own clubs, and you can't wear a wedding ring. The 70 nationwide chapters sponsor cookouts, mixers, and "fairway outings"—which, jokes founder and president Tom Alsop, have nothing to do with exposing gay golfers. "We're 4,000 individuals who happen to be single and play golf," he says. "We're a blend of everyone, from the wild and woolly to the recently widowed." Schneider is perhaps the wildest and woolliest; the rest tend to be fairly sedate pensioners out for a little match play.

For $70 a year, the ASGA gives you two rounds of golf, monthly newsletters, and invitations to five multichapter golf weekends—the most recent being the one Schneider attended in Savannah. New Jersey member Debbie Seaman calls these get-togethers "overnight camp for dysfunctional adults."

The dysfunctionals range in age from 30 to mid-70s, though the majority are between 45 and 60. Women slightly outnumber men. All can swing—a 25 handicap is average—but not all are swingers. "Twenty percent of the men ask for their own hotel rooms," says co-organizer Trista Holwager of North Carolina. "Either they want their privacy or they figure they'll get lucky."

Even bunkies get lucky, reports former Charlotte branch president Jackie Daly: "Sometimes, when you walk the lobbies at 2 a.m., you see which roommates have been thrown out of their room for awhile."

Nonetheless, Alsop insists, the association is not a dating service. "Sure," he concedes, "if one member is interested in another, the two can be paired for a round. But we don't set couples up. Nor are we a bunch of party animals out on the golf course. That comes later in the day."

Alsop figures the ASGA has accounted for about 70 weddings, one of which was held during a round at a club in Athens, Georgia. When the bride and groom reached the 18th green, they marked their balls, exchanged vows, kissed, and played out.

After two members married and had a child, Alsop received a baby picture with a note attached: "Even though he doesn't look like you, we feel you're responsible."

A divorced printing broker, Alsop conceived the ASGA by marrying his two favorite pastimes: golf and dating. "For me, church socials were too stifling," he says, "and singles bars were filled with smoke." The six charter members held their first meeting in 1991 in a Charlotte Shoney's. By 1994, the group had grown to 175. "Golf is a great way to check out potential mates," says Alsop, who met his girlfriend, Holwager, at an ASGA soiree in 1997. "Over four or five hours, you get to see them at their best and worst."

Golf offers every courting sand trap, from cheating to temper tantrums. The first woman Alsop was ever paired with kept telling him how good she was. "Then she teed off and woolly-wormed the ball to the green," he recalls. "It was 'Goddam this,' and 'Goddam that.' When she threw her clubs at the end of the first hole, I thought, Well, scratch that one off."

Scratching mates off was half the fun at the ASGA affair in Savannah. On Day 2, Branda Hall and Winona Ault rode to the course with fellow divorcé Bill Errikson. Hall sized up one of her male partners from Day 1: "He's been divorced 20 years, what does that tell you?"

"Nobody wants him," said Ault.

"Now, ladies, that's not necessarily true," Errikson piped in. "Maybe he hated marriage so much, he doesn't want to repeat the experience."

Many of the singles in Savannah seemed less interested in matrimony than in companionship. "At 60, marriage is a slower decision," said Alsop. "The kids don't want Daddy dividing up the assets with a total stranger."

Women looking for Mr. Right were just as likely to find Mr. Ed. Whiskey-swilling Ed Schneider and best buddy Jägermeister-guzzling Ed Holia were cruising their second national fairway outing. The Northern Kentuckians had last roomed together in December at the ASGA's Panama City, Florida, shindig, where they needed only 18 holes to drain an entire liter of Rebel Yell.

"We were drinkin' and partyin' and movin' and groovin'," recalls Schneider. "We did meet two nice gals from Illinois. But stuff didn't happen until after the event."

So how come the Illinois gals didn't follow you down to

Savannah?

"Hell, we didn't want them to. You don't bring a ham sandwich to a banquet." Chivalry will always have a dubious ally in Ed Schneider.

At the buffet banquet in the Savannah Marriott ballroom, singles flirted like idle gods. The men, in freshly pressed slacks and polo shirts, looked as if they had been licked clean by kittens; the women sparkled in pastel frocks as dainty as snowflakes.

"Sex!" howled Seaman, a fortyish New Jersey divorcé in a black leather skirt and fishnet stockings. "I didn't come here for *sex;* I didn't pack accordingly." Nor was she trawling for a hubby. "I have no interest in marrying an old golfer," she said. "Or an old pro golfer, even if, by chance, I knew who he was." Seaman is no Seniors Tour groupie: She thinks Gay Brewer is a niche magazine.

She and roomie Wanda Custer hung nicknames on the men in their foursomes: Billy Bear, Eveready Eddie, Bikin' Boy, Birdman, Chuckiepoo, Slut Muffin ... "I love 'em," said Custer. "They're all a pretty decent bunch of guys."

All except for the Maryland doctor who edged closer and closer to Seaman in their cart: "He was okay until he started telling me how his ex-wife ran off with the pool boy." Seaman edged farther and farther from him when he told her where in his ex-wife's anatomy he'd like to stick his 5-iron.

Racy repartee is essential to the singles golf mating ritual. "On the fairways," says Alsop, "there's often lots of talk about the birdies and the bees."

"More talk than action," says Holwager. "We're always

joking about putters, holes-in-one, and the back nine."

The constant chatter can affect a man's game. "In Panama City, I got stuck with three female yakkers," says Bob Webb, 68, of Tennessee. On the 1st tee, he shanked one into the trees. On the second, he sliced it into the water. After he fared no better at the third, one of the yakkers cackled: "I thought you could play. What's the matter?"

"*You're* the matter," snapped Webb. "Don't you ever shut up?"

Not long ago, a *Golf Digest Woman* survey revealed that while wives rank their husbands second only to friends among favorite golf partners, husbands would rather play with almost anyone *but* their spouses, who ranked ahead of only bosses. "The woman in my cart today gave me a headache from the second hole on," griped a dyspeptic divorcé who identified himself as Ed from Florida. "She wanted me to drive for her, caddy for her, rake the traps for her, give her compliments and emotional support. If she was the last woman left on earth and asked me to tie the knot, I'd still ask for a mulligan."

Tie the knot, and you're out of the ASGA. Alsop and Holwager are grappling with the impact marriage might have on their involvement with the group. "I mean, it *could* happen," says Alsop. "But it wouldn't look right," says Holwager. "It would be like a white guy running the NAACP."

Besides, nuptials always make Alsop sad. "Just hearing about the wedding of two club members brings tears to my eyes," he deadpans. "I don't cry because I'm happy for them. I cry because I'm losing their dues."

(PICNIC, LIGHTNING)

AVONDALE, PENNSYLVANIA

The late-afternoon sun slants low through the Osage orange trees off the 7th hole at the Inniscrone Golf Club, burnishing the sand traps with a soft, warm, wintry glow. Here in the mushroom country of Pennsylvania's Brandywine Valley, these mock oranges—battered by wind and scarred by lightning—flank the fairway like wounded veterans in a memorial parade for some forgotten hero.

Ripening "monkey brain" fruit hung from the branches in the summer of 2005 when John Needham popcorned a tee shot past the trees. The 45-year-old contractor was competing in a charity scramble to benefit the Tick Tock Early Learning Center in Avondale. The rain was between a mist and a drizzle—what the Irish call a mizzle—when a storm rumbled in and the sky darkened. Though groundkeepers darted from hole to hole blowing air horns and warning hackers to seek shelter, Needham and his group played on.

Needham, a passenger in a cart driven by his partner, John Skross, pulled up to a bunker. Needham stepped out and leaned down to pick up his ball. At that instant, there was a flash of lightning and a deafening boom of thunder. The blast of electricity knocked Skross off his feet and hurled him through the air. Needham crumpled to the ground. "The bolt was two feet wide and about as white as could be," recalls Boots Wilcox, another member of the foursome.

The lightning melted the gold chain around Needham's neck, fusing liquefied metal to the skin. His heart stopped. Skross and Matt Maloney, the group's fourth player, began CPR, but attempts to revive the fallen golfer failed. He was taken to a nearby hospital, where he was declared DOA. "It was a real freak of nature," says Wilcox. "On the news that night, Hurricane Schwartz, our local TV weatherman, said the bolt that hit John at Inniscrone was the only one in Chester County that day."

Of all sports, golf may be the most vulnerable to lightning. To a lightning bolt, a golf course is an open field. And a human being, particularly one holding a metal club and wearing metal spikes, is a ready lightning rod. On top of that, the game is played among trees and water, both of which attract lightning.

Lightning kills an average of 100 people and injures 500 annually in the United States. Five percent of the casualties occur on golf courses. "The electrical current searches for the shortest path to the ground, and in wide-open spaces, people are often the tallest conductors," says Dr. Phillip Yarnell, a senior member of the Lightning Data Center at St. Anthony Central Hospital in Denver. "When a group of people are hit on a course, usually one out of four suffers cardiac arrest."

Needham had been squatting on the berm of a hill. "Around here, we have a saying: Everyone has a lifetime clock," says Wilcox. "It doesn't matter what you're doing or where you are; when your time comes up, death is gonna get you. Even on the seventh fairway."

Major-championship winners Lee Trevino, Bobby Nichols, and Retief Goosen are among those who have survived strikes with relatively mild physical complications.

Trevino and Nichols were fried almost simultaneously during the 1975 Western Open in Illinois, prompting the Merry Mex's famous crack: "I should have held up a one-iron. Not even God can hit a one-iron."

Eleven years later, Goosen, then a 17-year-old amateur, was nearly killed by a strike in his native South Africa that left him with an irregular heartbeat, diminished hearing, and a pile of scorched clothes he still keeps in a drawer. All three pros are thankful for getting a mulligan in life.

THE MILLION-VOLT BOLT OF ENERGY THAT ZAPPED JERRY Heard on June 27, 1975, at Butler National not only shocked his central nervous system but short-circuited his PGA career. One of the most consistent players in the sport, he spiraled down like a Titleist circling a cup. Today, the golf Heard, 60, plays is mostly at night, in his dreams.

"I play a lot with Jack Nicklaus," says Heard, who won four tournaments in six seasons before the incident. "Not beating him, just competing." Heard will be on the tee but unable to find a place to put his ball in the ground; there's always something in his way. Or the Golden Bear will be calling his name on the tee—it's always the 1st tee at Riviera Country Club, way up at the top of a big hill—and Heard can't get there. Or Heard has too many clubs in his bag, and he's pulling them out frantically. "Weird stuff," he says. "Nothing like making a 40-footer to win the U.S. Open. I don't have that one."

Heard's Groundhog Night began recurring in 1975, when he and Trevino were huddled under an umbrella on the edge of the 13th green by Teal Lake, waiting for a shower to pass over. It was the second round of the Western Open, and the skies over Butler National were sunny and clear. Suddenly, lightning from a distant thunderstorm flashed sideways across the water and threw the two golfers into the air.

The most infamous lightning bolt in golfing history had surged through Trevino's bag and up his arm before exiting out his back. This was the *second* time Trevino had been lit up while playing golf. In case you were wondering, the odds of being struck are roughly one in 700,000 in a given year and one in 3,000 over the course of an 80-year lifetime. The chances of getting hit twice? One in 9,000,000.

Heard's point of entry was his groin, on which the tip of his umbrella had rested. (On the other side of the lake,

Nichols and Tony Jacklin were hit by a separate bolt.) Heard felt every muscle in his body roll up like a party favor. His hands clenched, and he couldn't open them. Heard had been so confident of his talent that he once quipped he could fall out of a car on the 1st tee at the start of every tournament and still make $100,000 a year. After being struck, he told himself: "I'll never play golf again."

Trevino and Nichols spent two nights in the hospital; Jacklin suffered only ringing in his ears. Because flooding on the course caused play to be suspended, Heard had all day Saturday to recover, and by Sunday he felt well enough to continue. Amazingly, he shot 72-73 in the final two rounds to finish fourth, five strokes behind winner Hale Irwin. Heard didn't realize the extent of his injuries until four weeks later, at the Canadian Open. There, Trevino told him, "My back's really hurting."

"So's mine," Heard replied.

They saw the same specialist. But while Trevino opted for back surgery, Heard got a second opinion: Rest and hope for the best. He did.

Eventually, Heard was bedridden for three months and sat out most of the '76 season, during which his wife divorced him. He returned to the Tour in 1977 and played in pain, trying to find a swing that didn't hurt. His back went out while he was playing in an event in Japan. In the months that followed, he grew fat and irritable. "I used to wake up and I'd be in a good mood," he says. "Then I started waking up and my back hurt."

As it turned out, the lightning had damaged Heard's

spinal cord and cauterized nerve endings in the tissue. Despite constant twinges, he won the 1978 Atlanta Golf Classic. He still couldn't get through a full shot, so he hit slap-hooks around the Atlanta Country Club, but he made a bunch of putts and finished 19-under. Figuring the victory was a fluke, Heard finally had the operation that had helped Trevino. "It relieved a lot of aches," he says.

Trevino won nine more tournaments on the PGA Tour, but Heard never regained his form. He couldn't hit a cut the way he used to, and he had never been good at tinkering with his swing, even in his prime. "Jerry was a guy who played very instinctively," says Nicklaus.

The once preternaturally cocky Heard became afraid to swing. He quit the Tour in 1980. Three years later, broke and living in North Carolina, he heard about an opening as director of golf at South Seas Plantation on Captiva Island, Florida. Heard used a friend's credit card to call the club, then borrowed cash from his parents to pay his airfare. He was hired and stayed for almost two decades.

FEW LIGHTNING STORMS HAVE SWEPT OVER A MAJOR championship tournament with such frightening intensity as the one that disrupted the 1991 U.S. Open. The sky, implacable, walked on stilts of rain, and forked lightning splayed theatrically on opening day at Hazeltine National in Chaska, Minnesota, near Minneapolis. More than 40,000 people were on the heavily wooded course when the rain started to fall in swaying curtains, and many took cover under the trees.

A half-dozen spectators stood side by side under a 30-foot weeping willow near the 11th tee, one of the lowest spots at Hazeltine. "With its canopy, that willow looked like a great umbrella," recalls Ray Gavin, one of the six. "When I was running to the tree, I saw lots of people under a giant oak and hundreds more who refused leave the metal bleachers. I thought, Those fools are going to get hit by lightning."

Two quick cracks of thunder later, Gavin and the others under the willow fell like duckpins. "Actually, we didn't fall," says Gavin's friend John Hannahan. "We melted." A bolt had deflected off the tree and jumped to the six bystanders. The lightning had penetrated Gavin's shoulder and exited through his hip. It came into Hannahan through one foot and out through the other.

Gavin, now a 66-year-old retired sales manager, was knocked unconscious. When he came to, parademics were putting him on a gurney. "It dawned on me that from the neck down, I couldn't move," he says. "Not my toes, not my feet, not my hands. I thought I was paralyzed. I thought, My God, I'm going to be a burden to my family forever." Happily, the feeling in his body returned within six hours.

Hannahan, a 60-year-old real estate appraiser, remembers looking out onto the 16th fairway. Then came a bright light. And a hollow expression on the face of the young man lying nearest the willow's trunk. That man was Billy Fadell, a computer technician whose father had worked as a course marshal the day before. Fadell, 28, was pronounced dead at a nearby hospital, the first-ever lightning fatality at a PGA Tour-sanctioned event.

Meanwhile, Hannahan's heart had stopped, but he was revived by a volunteer fireman at the scene. He stirred, briefly, in the ambulance, where he was told that he had been hit by lightning and might be singed. He raised his head groggily, lifted the sheet in which he was wrapped, and surveyed his naked body. "Good," Hannahan mumbled. "Nothing's burned down there." He wasn't totally conscious until he woke up in ER, 45 minutes later. "I looked at the end of my bed and saw my priest, my doctor and my wife," he says. "I thought, this is not good."

But it wasn't too bad. Hannahan and Gavin got better quickly, though there were aftereffects. "My wife was upset that I didn't have an out-of-body experience," Hannahan deadpans. "The truth is, I had an erection for six months."

Like Walt Whitman, Gavin's neighbors still sing the body electric: "Whenever their car batteries need to be charged," he cracks, "they drop by my house and clamp jumper cables to my hips."

HEARD HAS DEVELOPED A DARK SENSE OF HUMOR TOO. Since 2000, he has been part owner of Silverthorn Country Club, the hub of a retirement community in southwest Florida. Most days after work, he fishes for bass in the water hazard on the 9th hole with his schnauzer, Miles. "Jerry could've been a superstar," Trevino once said, but Heard says he could happily spend the rest of his days mixing it up with his members, fishing with Miles, and dreaming of Nicklaus.

Just one hitch, he says: "We get a lot of lightning here."

LILLIPUT-PUTT

MYRTLE BEACH, SOUTH CAROLINA

Most miniature golf courses are so sublimely surreal that only Salvador Dalí could run the pro shops. What other sport requires you to slap a ball between the whirling blades of a windmill, then through a papier-mâché sphinx, and into the jaws of a giant toad with revolving eyes? Somewhere in the world, there must be a course with a melting watch.

Surely no sport is so unremittingly Grimm. Mini golf was first played in 1926 at a Tennessee resort called Fairyland Inn, where plaster gnomes and elves guarded the holes. By the end of the Roaring '20s, little links carpeted the country and had spawned a hit song, "I've Gone Goofy Over Miniature Golf." Some players did just that: A course was laid out on the grounds of a state hospital for the insane.

Miniature golf courses were installed on Manhattan rooftops, in hotel ballrooms, on the decks of battleships. One California woman sued her zoning board for permission to put a course in a graveyard on her land, with tombstones as hazards. There was even a course in Vienna's Prater Gardens—perhaps best known for the Ferris wheel scene in *The Third Man*. Imagine Orson Welles selling black-market penicillin while putting into a 20-foot Sacher torte.

The game survives into the 21st century with a retro-hipness. Jumbo "miniature golf parks"—with easy, channeled fairways and indented greens—carpet the country. But for the real deal you've got to go to Myrtle Beach, a drowsy hamlet that bills itself as the miniature golf capital of the world. Most of the Lilliput-putt action in Vanna White's hometown lies along the Grand Strand, a garish strip of hermit crab emporiums and gifts shops, whose names—The Curious Mermaid, The Gay Dolphin—sound like seafaring porn flicks. The same goes for Three-Ball Charlie, an oddity at the Ripley's Believe It or Not Museum. Museum propaganda claims that Three-Ball could "insert a tennis ball, billiard ball, and golf ball side by side in his mouth and whistle at the same time."

Three-Ball could very well be the patron saint of Myrtle Beach, where nearly every mini golf course has the bullyragging absurdism of Monty Python. In the Pythonian scheme of things, people are either sensible, slightly silly, silly, or very silly. In the early 1990s, I flew down to Myrtle Beach with a slightly silly friend, John Diliberto, a bluff, bearded radio host with trampoline eyebrows; and a silly one, Mark Moskowitz, a political consultant who lives by the ethic "Perseverance despite pointlessness." Over a single crazed weekend, we played all 30 of the town's putt-putt courses.

WE BEGAN AT INLET ADVENTURE. IT'S A LITTLE AFTER 8 a.m., and the only thing open is the sky: Rain pours down. We tee off at 8:30 and start arguing at 8:32. Moskowitz has calculated how fast we need to play to get through 16 courses by midnight. "Making allowances for driving and eating," he says, "we've got 45 minutes at each one, max."

"Are you kidding?" says Diliberto, the purist. "You can't play faster than the people in front of you."

"We'll play holes out of order," says Moskowitz, the pragmatist.

A more pressing question arises after Moskowitz wins this mountainous, waterfall-filled course by five strokes. Tapping figures into the laptop computer he has brought along to track our progress, he asks, "Is this a pirate course?"

"What's the difference?" I say.

"I've got to list it under a theme. Pirate? Mountain? Nautical?"

"Nautical has a nice ring to it."

"Pirate?" says Diliberto, arching his trampolines. "Where's the treasure chest? I don't see crow's nests. I don't see doubloons." He might have a point. A Jolly Roger does not a pirate course make. Or does it?

ADVENTURE FALLS

Having won the first two matches with orange balls, Moskowitz switches to yellow. "I'll be able to see better in the caves," he explains. The cave on 15 has an unadvertised water hazard—a poor putt will dump your ball into a puddle. This tricky par-2 must be played billiards style. Diliberto's brown ball banks off a couple of rails and stops on the soggy carpet about three feet from the cup. Moskowitz's yellow ball follows a similar route and sidles up to Diliberto's. My red ball flies down the fairway with the force of a sledgehammer break. It hits the other two, and all three go spinning off like planets. Red lands in the hole; yellow and brown, the drink. The air is damp and fusty. I wonder if a Neanderthal swung the first club in a cave like this—not at a ball, but at another Neanderthal.

JUNGLE GOLF

To paraphrase P.G. Wodehouse, the old-timer handing out putters is either a man of about 150 who's rather young for his years or a man of about 110 who's been aged by trouble. He says a customer once told him the course is the oldest in Myrtle Beach. "How do you know for sure?" asked the old-timer skeptically.

"Because I designed it," said the customer proudly.

"Is that a fact?" said the old-timer. "Ever give any thought to drainage?"

The small lakes swamping the first five greens were not left by an incontinent plaster zebra. As we slosh through the back nine, the old-timer yells, "How many holes in one did you get? Most people get three or four, but one fella had 14."

Diliberto lowers his head and whispers, "Did I get *any*?"

He comes from four strokes back to overtake me on 16. "It smells like victory," he screams after bogeying 18. Either victory or Gracie, the African pygmy goat penned at the 1st tee.

HURL ROCK

A green. A rock. A sunken cup. The 15th hole is as spare as the stage in a Beckett play. At the end of the green is the cup. Behind the cup is the rock. No doglegs, no dips, no rises, no looming Buddhas, no overlapping octopus tendrils. Just pure, nihilistic mini golf. "This should be a cinch," says Moskowitz. It's not. His shot skirts the cup and stops behind the rock. He settles for a par 3. As does Diliberto. As do I. And you thought Beckett held the patent on the grim futility of human endeavor.

BUCCANEER BAY

The cashier gives us a choice. "You can play either the East or the West Isles," she says. "Your East Isles has your international speed carpet and your cave. Your West Isles is a little more aggressive, and you go over the falls."

We side with aggression, which is fine with Moskowitz, who is eyeing his watch. "We averaged 49.3 minutes on the last three courses," he frets. "Let's play this as fast as we can." We buzz through the holes, shouting our scores to

Moskowitz across the empty West Isles links-cape like revved-up country auctioneers. "Three!" "Two!" "Four!" "Two!" "Did I hear four?" "Five."

Twelve minutes after teeing off, we reach the 18th hole.

Diliberto: "That wasn't fun."

Moskowitz: "We can have fun on some of them if we rush through most of them."

Five dizzying hours later, Moskowitz's face is glazed with the unmistakable blankness that occurs when one game begins to blend with the next. Eyeballs spinning in their sockets like roulette wheels, attention waning, he scales the skull of a gigantic gorilla and watches his turquoise Titleist bounce off a brick bumper and down a tunnel, then lazily wind around a path and into the cup. "Haven't we played his hole before?" he says.

We had, and we would again. "I don't even take in the scenery anymore," Moskowitz says on Day 2 during a breather at Aladdin's Magic Springs. "We're already on 14, and I just noticed the genie at the entrance."

Diliberto says, "There is no genie at the entrance."

"See what I mean?"

We play both the front and the back courses, aptly named The Front and The Back. Diliberto takes The Front, Moskowitz takes The Back. At lunch, I take The Check.

Moskowitz has begun to time everything: course time, hole time, travel time, even rest-stop time. Now in the restaurant, he's clocking our waitress. "She's taking forever to bring the check," he fumes. "We could have played three courses!" Ahead by 22 strokes, Moskowitz has begun to crack.

By the time we reach Treasure Island, the crack has widened to a chasm. His face turns ashen after his faded orange ball stops dead an inch from the opening hole. "I know I maligned it," he says just above a whisper.

"Who's it?" I ask.

"Orange," he says. Except for that one regrettable interlude at Adventure Falls, Moskowitz has played bright orange exclusively. "I didn't want to take faded orange," he confesses, "but that's all this place has. I know in my heart that faded orange is no good. But I'm afraid if I pick another color, bright orange will know and lose faith in me. So I'm sticking with orange—no matter what shade—until the very end."

Which he does.

Astonishingly, after 540 holes of putting through tepees, over cement salamanders in suspenders, under the legs of 30-foot Tyrannosauruses, beside gurgling streams dyed Ty-D-Bol blue, and up three-tiered mesas concealed by frogs brandishing golf umbrellas, we were all within five strokes of each other. "We all live in a miniature golf course," Moskowitz began his victory speech. "To survive, you've got to grind it out."

We shuffle out to the car. I slip behind the steering wheel, turn the key, and coast blissfully down the Grand Strand. I slow down on curves. I speed up on straightaways. I narrowly miss a truck stalled in the middle of the road. Like a mini golf ball, I, too, am a hapless commuter, propelled by the pitch of the path around me.

"Hey, look!" shouts Diliberto. "I think I see a giant clown up ahead. You think maybe we missed a course?"

We whiz by the polka-dot clown, the lime-green waffle house, the cherry-red motor home, and lots of other wacky roadside ticky-tacky.

Moskowitz was right. The world *is* a miniature golf course.

THE THREE OF US HAD PLANNED A 10TH-ANNIVERSARY rematch, but at the last minute, Diliberto bugged out, and Moskowitz flat out refused to come. Perhaps they'd become adults. "Be that way," I snarled. "I'm going anyway." To keep the threesome from becoming a lonesome onesome, I recruited my then-11-year-old daughter, Daisy, whose height —5'1"—qualified her as a genuine miniature golfer.

I figured three days of mini golf might be a hard sell to a sixth-grader, so I played up the storybook angle. I raved about Spyglass Adventure's exploding powder kegs, gangplanks, and smoking cannons. But Daisy was unmoved. I rabbited on about the catapults, battering rams, and sorcerer's cave at McLean's Medieval Village. Daisy still wouldn't bite. I rhapsodized about the sublime surrealism of Wacky Golf, which came about as close to the original Fairyland as you can get.

The wackiest hole, I told her, is not the one that requires you thump a ball between the whirling blades of a windmill erected in Mother Hubbard's shoe, then through a papier-mâché troll and into the mouth of an enormous amberjack with revolving eyes. No, I said, the wackiest hole is the one monitored by Wacky Man, an ear-shaped mutant even Dr. Seuss wouldn't have delivered.

"Well, all right," Daisy said at last. "You convinced me to go."

"What clinched it?" I asked excitedly. "The gangplanks, the catapults, the amberjack ..."

"Actually, it was none of them. It was when you said I could get off school."

And so, just before Thanksgiving, we played hooky, hopped a plane, and landed in Myrtle Beach. Sadly, a half-dozen courses are closed for the season, and another half-dozen are closed, period. Wacky Golf is now an abandoned lot choked with weeds and whiskey bottles. The two-story giraffe that once grazed near the 3rd hole has loped off, the giant orange toad at 11 has bounded away, and the wand-waving wizard at 15 has disappeared. Only the concrete tepee at 17 remains. While Daisy waits at the gate, I look within and see a homeless man—smelly, dirty, and cloaked in Astroturf—beating his head against the wall.

"What was inside?" asks Daisy.

"A real wacky man."

We drive on and stop at Dragon's Lair Fantasy Golf, a course laid out on the parapets of a magnificent ersatz castle. The head of a huge, fire-belching monster emerges from one of the turrets every few minutes, and the scorecard reads: "Should thy ball go out of bounds, replace it where it went out, and give thyself a one-stroke penalty."

"Dost thou understandeth the rules?" I ask Daisy.

"Verily," she says, putting on a wry face. "Let's pretend we're in a fairy tale, and that the courses are enchanted, and that we're on a quest."

"Okay, but what quest?"

"Why, to play every course, of course."

On the final hole, with Daisy down four strokes, comes such a rattling of the skies and lumbering of the earth as never was. Under the hot, glaring eyes of the Lair's dragon, she takes her club, strikes her salmon Top-Flite with a mighty swing, and lo! It bounds around the green, ricochets off the rails, boomerangs off a boulder, skips over the sidewalk, and rolls noisily across the parking lot toward Kings Highway. Daisy bids me fetch the ball from its place of horror, and (verily) I do.

"One-stroke penalty," I say.

"Practice swing," she says and, raising the club yet again, smites the ball. And lo! It passes through many windings and turnings and trickles into the cup for an ace. I follow. Six times my ball climbs a hillock. Six times it rolls back to the tee. Daisy rejoices, exceedingly. "I win by one," she roars from the ramparts. And I am left to bellow forth my lamentable complaints to senseless stones.

And so we set forth, as knights errant, to seek more putt-putt adventure. At Pirate's Watch, Daisy acts out a mini-golf version of *Goldilocks and the Three Bears*. She picks out a blue ball, but that is too scratched for her. She picks out a pink ball, but that is too shiny for her. She picks out a ball the color of ballpark mustard that is neither too scratched nor too shiny, but just right. Then she picks out a putter. The first one is too long; the second too short; and the third is neither too short nor too long, but just right.

Thirty minutes later, with the game on the line, Daisy crouches near the scuttled ship's mainmast and mulls which of the three chutes to aim for. "I'll try the middle," she says and, wielding her club like a freebooter's cutlass, raps her coal-black Maxfli chuteward. The ball lips the chute on the far right, circles the chute on the far left, and swirls into the middle one, which spits it into the cup. "Ah!" says Daisy. "Just right."

Over the next eight hours we surmount many hazards: sand, water, and, at Hawaiian Rumble Golf, the Pampers some mini mini-golfer left in the middle of the fairway. We travel far and we travel fast, and we travel east and west, north and south. We travel 'til dusk, when Daisy's strength is almost finished. The two of us call it a night at Jurassic Golf, a putt-putt park for people who think Fred Couples is a Bedrock dating service. With the scorecard in her back pocket and a runty yellow pencil clenched between her teeth, she watches her purple Pinnacle bounce off a brick bumper and down a tunnel, then lazily wind around a path and into the cup. "Haven't we played his hole before?" she says.

We resume the following morning. We play in palaces and plains and plateaus. We play in the darksome depths of a thick jungle. We play in the cavernous mountains and the mountainous caverns of Mayday Golf, where the main attraction—a nose-diving Lockheed PV-2 Harpoon—gives new dimension to the phrase "crash course." You're supposed to yell "Mayday!" if your ball slices into a waterfall. Mine does, but I don't.

Our quest ends at Mt. Atlanticus, a $3 million indoor/outdoor facility that could have been created by the set designer of *A Nymphoid Barbarian in Dinosaur Hell*. Outside, the course climbs up and up to the third floor of a thatched hut. Inside, the walls are hung with paintings of extinct creatures and prehistoric cave babes. Dangling from the ceiling are dozens of video monitors on which a tweedy gent who calls himself Sir Jiggy Mountebank drones on endlessly about the lost continent of Atlantis. The sign in front of the cash register says "Minotaur Goff." Behind it sits an elderly man in a coat of armor—a refugee from Fairyland, perhaps.

"What's minotaur goff?" I ask.

"Down here, people don't say 'golf,' " he explains. "They say, 'Let's go play some goff.' "

I nod.

The old knight informs us that Mt. Atlanticus was discovered by a mysterious mino-goff visionary. "On March 29, 1998, he sighted a land mass two miles offshore from Myrtle Beach Pavilion," he says. "A couple of days later, the mass settled here, two blocks from the ocean."

Daisy nods.

"The mass he sighted was a minotaur goff island resort, some 60,000 years old. It had broken off the sunken continent of Atlantis and, over thousands of years, drifted to the Carolina coast."

We both nod.

"According to our visionary founder, minotaur goff was outlawed at least seven times in Atlantican history. So many citizens played so much of the time that the civilization began to crumble. Stores and factories were empty, babies perished unsuckled in their cribs, crops rotted on their vines as the Atlanticans putted and putted and putted ..."

We both begin to nod off.

I say: "Does this visionary live in Myrtle Beach?"

He says: "Goes and comes."

"Does he ever come around?"

"In and out."

"Can you possibly be any vaguer?"

"Maybe yes, maybe no."

To fully appreciate minotaur goff, you need to smoke an herb not sold in the Mt. Atlanticus pro shop. We play it straight and eventually arrive at the 18th hole, a long, ever-narrowing peninsula with a cup at the end. A hole-in-one gets you a lifetime pass. My hurried shot hugs the carpet for 10 feet before veering into the abyss. Daisy takes her time. But just as she finishes her backswing, the old knight appears. Spooked, she slams her avocado Acushnet into the bottomless chasm.

I'd told Daisy there would be days like this. But I'd forgotten to warn her about the knights.

HOME ON THE RANGE

ORLANDO, FLORIDA

Jim Reid doesn't wear his bulletproof vest to bed anymore. But he still keeps a bowie knife hidden in his boot, a Colt .45 stashed in his Corvette and a 9mm Beretta concealed somewhere on his body. "I prefer my 9mm Beretta to my .380 Beretta," Reid says. "The nine-millimeter holds 16 bullets. The .380 only holds 13. In my line of work you can never be too sure."

You wouldn't think that finding and selling wayward golf balls was such a perilous profession. But as Reid tells it, there's enough danger and underwater intrigue in the golf ball-recycling business to sustain a James Bond sequel.

"Basically, I profit from other people's mistakes," says Reid, whose outfit, Second Chance, based in Orlando, Florida, brings in tens of millions of dollars a year. He worries about operations horning in on his turf. He worries about poachers raiding his ponds at night. He worries about alligators and sabotage and industrial espionage. "I used to be paranoid," he says, smoothing back his Elvis-eque pompadour. "But now I'm cured. Now I'm just . . . careful."

Reid arrived in Orlando in 1966 and took a job as a surveyor at Walt Disney World. One day a friend of his who was the pro at a nearby country club told Reid he thought there might be a lot of balls in one of the course's water hazards. Reid dived in and discovered "the bottom of the pond was covered with golf balls—white gold!"

He gave up surveying and plunged into ball salvaging. Soon his garage was crowded with Spaldings and Pinnacles and Maxflis and Top-Flites and Acushnets. He washed them in an old Maytag and resold them to the hapless souls who had hit them into the pond in the first place.

Now Reid and the 10 divers he employs comb ponds all over Florida, the state that boasts the most golf courses and most lost balls in the country. His divers recovered six million balls last year alone. Each ball is cleaned in a vat of mysterious, stain-removing chemicals. Reid is so leery of spies that he makes employees sign a five-page contract, promising never to reveal the solution's formula.

After immersion in Reid's golf dip, the balls are dried in plastic crates and graded and sorted according to brand and general condition. Then they're repainted, clearcoated and packed off to pro shops and driving ranges, where the cycle starts all over again. The average cost of the reconditioned balls is $325 per 500-ball box.

Actually, Second Chance is something of a misnomer, as most balls have more than two lives. The covering of choice used to be balata, a soft substance that would cut easily or cause balls to "go out of round" quickly. But several years ago manufacturers started using Surlyn, a synthetic substance that provides a harder, more durable jacket. Now even cut balls can be rehabilitated for driving range use. The lowest-grade cut balls go to cruise ships, from which they're hit into the ultimate water hazard.

Reid perfected his refinishing technique the way a hacker hones his stroke, through trial and error. He once let 500 range balls clunk around a cement mixer overnight. "They rolled and rolled and rolled," he says. "It took everything off." Including the better part of the dimples.

Unfortunately, he forgot to tell this to the golf pro to whom he sold the balls. The pro called him a few days later. Reid says he sounded perplexed. "What's with those balls?" asked the pro. "They've been loop-de-looping all afternoon."

Reid mentioned the cement mixer.

"No problem," said the pro. "It's been great for business. People have been signing up for lessons all morning."

Reid has clients in most states and dozens of countries. But his domain is dwarfed by that of another Floridian, Jerry Gunderson. "Jerry is like Idi Amin," Reid says with sly amusement. "He wants to control the world."

He means the world of used golf balls. Gunderson once approached Reid with an offer to buy Second Chance. International Golf, Gunderson's company, is headquartered in a sprawling Deerfield Beach, Florida, complex that's ringed with barbed wire. Security is so tight that you have to be buzzed into the boss's office.

Nine years older than Reid, Gunderson is an effusive fellow with a firm handshake and a belly shaped like an outsize Hogan 392. His business card is stamped with the motto "No fuss, no muss, leave the golf ball diving to us." He shells out about $500,000 a year for exclusive scouring rights to 600 courses from Maine to California, including almost every TPC layout. On a good day his divers can pull up as many as 1,500 balls. He says the water hazards on the right side of the fairway yield the most balls. "Most golfers slice shots," he says. "Very few hook them."

Gunderson was 12 when he waded into his first pond, at a muni in Lake Worth. He laid out his booty on a bench and sold the entire haul. "I may have been a little too industrious," he says. "They put a detective on my tail and caught me in the act." So he struck a deal with the club pro, who paid him 8 cents for each recovered ball.

He paid his way through Florida State by tending a small circuit of courses in Jacksonville, St. Pete, and Atlanta. Fraternity brothers who wanted a piece of Gunderson's action had to pass a test: "I made them stand under a freezing shower for 20 minutes." Few survived the initiation.

Before investing in scuba gear, Gunderson groped around in the cold, silty sludge with his toes. "In the old days I walked into a lot of glass jugs," he recalls. "I'd yank my toes out and my feet would be slashed. The great thing today is that there are no glass bottles. Now it's all cans."

But the hazards faced by contemporary ball hawks are

far more formidable. "You can't make out anything," says Reid, who was once singed by lightning while submerged. "Your hands begin to see, like a blind man reading Braille." Two of Reid's divers have been bitten by alligators or thumped by their tails; another gave up a finger to a snapping turtle. Another lost an eye when he popped out of the water and into the trajectory of a 3-wood. Others have drowned.

Besides balls and clubs, divers dredge up all sorts of nongolfing debris, such as 10-speed bicycles, tire irons, and X-rated videocassettes. One ball-retriever in Ohio found a dead man with his feet in cement blocks and his hands chained behind him. "I doubt that the victim was caught poaching balls," says Gunderson. "The punishment seems too severe."

Poachers, known as nighthawks, are the recycling trade's greatest handicap. By raking away balls, they rake off profits. "The most common kind are the retirees who buy $800,000 homes along the water," he says. "They feel they're entitled to the balls. They're pirates, in my view."

And how do ball manufacturers view recyclers? "They leave us alone," he says. "They realize there's room enough for both of us." The used-ball market, he says, is just a little dimple on the face of an industry that sells a billion new balls a year.

Reid doesn't worry that sporting goods firms may one day conspire with officials to wipe out the good-old-ball network. "About the only thing they could do to stop us," he says, "is change the rules and make all golf balls float. But, then, that would hurt their business too."

THE EVERYHACKER

AZLE, TEXAS

I t's one thing for a golfer to be booed by the gallery, quite another to be mooed. But there was Robert Landers swinging a sand wedge in the pasture behind his house to a bovine ovation. Landers's Legion—five heifers and a calf—chewed over his follow-through with contented countenances.

"Out here, a ball that lands on a cow patty is not an unplayable lie," says Landers as he hits from a dung heap. "You can tell when your ball hits one 'cause it won't bounce a bit." Has there ever been a more unorthodox chip shot?

Landers was uncowed and unbowed during the 1995 Senior PGA Tour qualifying tournament in Lutz, Florida. Wearing sneakers, lugging a garage-sale carry bag and wielding a set of glue-and-go clubs he'd bought from his cousin Steven Sosebee for $70, Landers, a hardscrabble Texas farmer, shot a 73 in the final round. His four-over-par 288 tied him for sixth place, earning him $4,270. Even better, it earned him a berth on the 1996 Senior Tour, where he competed against the likes of Ray Floyd and Dave Stockton for $1 million purses.

"Just eight of the 111 entrants won full exemptions," says club pro Steve Champion. "Seven of the eight were either playing pros or solid club pros. Robert was the only one who needed the purse money to play on the Tour."

Of the handful of steelworkers, mechanics, and insurance salesmen to have qualified for the senior circuit since its inception in 1980, none has followed a more unlikely path than Landers, who has been trying to eke out a living on his farm since the clothing store he managed went bust two years ago. He has spent much of his free time—and there's been lots of it—chopping wood, raising cattle, and honing his game in his pasture. "The cows come in handy," Landers says. "They keep the grass down."

As plain and solid as an oak plank, Landers is a simple, practical man who may be slow to act but is unswerving when he does. Before Lutz, the most Landers had won in a tournament was $700, at the Texoma Senior Open earlier this year. "Imagine, $700!" he says guilelessly. "I was so happy, I didn't sleep for a week."

At 50, he saw his life changed by the lavish Senior tour, mostly in ways he didn't care to think about. "How we're gonna deal with this deal I got us into, I don't know," Landers says before it all began. "I don't even know how to get to those tournament cities, or where they are."

He hates planes and hasn't flown since 1981. "Truth is, I didn't have time to consider what I'd done," says Landers. "The whole thing was like a fairy tale. Cinderella, maybe."

His wife, Freddie, demurs. "Except that Cinderella knew her stepsisters had fine things and that she was entitled to fine things," she says. "We were contented where we was at. In our wildest dreams, if we was gonna dream a dream, it wouldn't be this big. Our dream was that we weren't gonna get any worse off. We were just a couple of nobodies from nowhere."

Nowhere is about 18 miles northwest of Fort Worth. It's called Azle, and you could clear downtown with a 7-iron. "I lived in Fort Worth for 10 years, but it was too fast for me," Landers says. "Being out here with the trees, the birds, the creek, and the dirt is the best life I could ever imagine."

He moseys around his dung-dotted practice range, pointing out the landmarks. Large plywood cutout cows are scattered over the pasture. "Over that way is Dino's Cliff," Landers says, indicating the short precipice where a calf named Dino once slid into a ditch. "There's Jenn's Gulley," he says, wagging a finger at the culvert Jenn the heifer plunged into. "Want to see Willie's corner?" Poor Willie was his beloved dog, who met his end between the blades of a mower and was replaced by a mutt named Oleo.

"Why did you bring another dog home?" demanded Freddie.

"Reason is," Robert said, "if I'm out cuttin' wood and a tree falls and kills me, I need something to say goodbye to."

Robert and Freddie met in 1975 at Mitchell's department store in Azle. He was the manager; she was a clerk. "I was dustin' some purses when I first laid eyes on Robert," recalls Freddie. "I thought, Oh, he is so good-lookin'. Of course, we were married to different people then."

They became friends but not intimates. Then Freddie's son died in a car crash, and her husband left her for a younger woman. Robert says his own wife "hated golf, hated guns, hated me." He would skulk around town, digging his hands deeply enough into his pockets to scratch his knees. "Freddie and I realized we had a lot in common," he says. "We were both thrown-away people."

Tears formed in Landers's eyes as he related all this at the farmhouse dinner table. Freddie had set out steaming bowls of corn, peas, and mashed potatoes. Robert jabbed a fork into a heap of brisket. "This is Gus," he tells a visitor. "He was an ornery little calf, so he's probably tough."

The kitchen decor is Early Holstein, with cow clocks, cow cookie jars, cow pot holders, cow soap dispensers, cow teapots, cow planters, cow refrigerator magnets—even cow bowling pins. Since Freddie lost her assembly-line job, she has carved out a slender living painting cows on old tenpins. "I sell them at flea markets every Monday," says Robert. "In these parts, everybody collects cows."

Their collection of live cows runs to 45. Robert and Freddie bought their first calves in 1988 at Smelley's Dairy in nearby Springtown. "Freddie and I didn't know anything about milking them," says Robert. "So I'd milk the right side, and she'd milk the left."

Freddie christened each calf. "If they didn't have names," Robert says, "we wouldn't know who we was talkin' about." There was Spooky, Daisy, Rocky, Dino, and Hope. "Hope was sick," says Freddie, "and we hoped she'd live."

The herd grew with the addition of Sundance and Teensy and Wobbles and Peekaboo and Dirtsy. "Another's called Moolah, because we're gonna have some money now," says Freddie, who thinks up names faster than a bad-check artist at a teller's window.

As a kid Robert couldn't afford to play golf. He was 22 when his uncle Foster taught him the basics. He scraped together enough for a driver, a sand wedge, and a Patty Berg 8-iron. A year later he got his first putter.

He started to play seriously in 1972, always on muni courses. He qualified for the U.S. Open and the U.S. Amateur in 1980, missing the cut in both, and twice was the low amateur at the Texas Open. However, a pinched sciatic nerve curtailed his career, and he stopped playing competitively in 1981 to ease the pain that made his left leg go numb. The move to the country in 1987 proved salubrious. "Farm life strengthened me," he says. "After building fences, hauling hay, and splitting logs, golf does not hurt."

Landers got to thinking about the Senior Tour in 1991 and prepared for it with a sense of sacrifice and stern calling. He played the Texas Barbecue Circuit, a series of two-round tournaments run by civic groups in small towns. Most other days he would wallop balls in the pasture, walk after them and wallop them back. Sixty thousand practice balls a year. Finally Freddie said, "Either you're gonna play, or you're gonna get a job."

So Robert composed a letter to friends and local business people about backing him in his effort to join the Senior Tour. The prospective said, in part, "I will work hard, and there will be winnings."

But he never sent the letter out. "Forget everybody," Freddie told him. "You're gonna do it on your own."

To cover the $2,000 entry fee for the Senior Tour qualifying tournament, Robert cashed in an IRA. Also, some buddies at a nine-hole muni where he plays put out a jug. "We raised 50 bucks," says Champion, who owns and teaches at the Casino Beach Golf Academy, in Fort Worth. "Robert graciously accepted."

After successfully competing at the regional qualifier in San Antonio, Landers advanced to the finals. Or more precisely, puttered. He and Freddie made the 1,300-mile trip to Lutz in their 1989 Chevy.

Playing in his muddy Reeboks, Landers cut an unimposing figure. He wouldn't wear the new FootJoy golf shoes that Freddie made him buy, because he hadn't worn spikes in more than five years and thought he would scuff the greens if he dragged his feet. "Everybody in Lutz knew us as the Farmers from Azle," says Freddie, who rode in the cart with Robert, wearing a bandage on her nose because Sundance had kicked her in the face. "We looked plenty pitiful, but nobody treated us ugly."

Fighting headwinds up to 40 mph that were the result of tropical storm Gordon, Landers shot an opening-round

72, which put him in a tie for fourth. "Gordon helped me a lot," he says. "I can keep the ball down and control it. Some golfers shot themselves out. They couldn't handle the weather."

Much less the competition. "Q-School is the toughest event I've ever played in," says veteran Senior Tour player Rocky Thompson, a 40-year pro. "If a man is good enough to get one of the eight spots, he should succeed. On the other hand, I've seen some talented qualifiers not play to their capabilities when they're upside the Trevinos, the Stocktons, and the Floyds. They get too excited. You've got to be pretty sure of your game."

Which Landers is. "I've always been very insecure," he says. "Golf gave me greater self-esteem. I'm now to the point where I feel equal to the next guy."

In this case, equal is more steady than exciting. "I'm not much into risk," Landers says. Nor is he much into sand or water. Over 72 holes in Lutz, Landers hit into only two bunkers and two ponds.

He relied on a reconditioned 3-wood, which has a graphite shaft he found in a garbage can. "Robert spent $12 on that club," says his friend Jerry Hamilton. "That's really extravagant for him."

Landers wasn't being cheap, just frugal. He used a coupon that got him and Freddie into a Ramada Inn for $34 a night. During the entire 10-day trip, they spent $69.35 on gas, $4.59 on Advil, and $147.75 on food and other necessities. "We would have spent less," says Landers, apologetically, "but we had to buy a couple of pillows for my back."

In Lutz, he used only seven balls over four rounds. "I would have used fewer," he says, "if the two hadn't landed in the drink." He had intended to use the same ball the entire final round but reconsidered when he double-bogeyed the 15th. "By golly, using a new ball turned out to be a good move," he says. "I parred the last three holes."

After Robert qualified for the Tour with a short putt on 18, he and Freddie embraced. And cried. And embraced. And cried. But they didn't futz around Lutz. "I had to get back to Azle to chop firewood," Robert says. "I had promised some folks I would have it for them by Thanksgiving."

So how did Robert and Freddie celebrate? "On the drive home," says Robert, "we stopped at a Waffle House instead of a McDonald's."

"And Robert left the waitress a $2 tip!" says Freddie.

Alas, Landers lasted only two years on the 50s circuit. The swing that Farmer Bob honed among the Holsteins held up fine, but his putting gave him a cow. Golf's Everyhacker made a little hay on the tour—$158,240, which allowed him to pay off his mortgage, buy a tractor and a pickup truck, and dole out cash to the needy in Azle.

"It sure was exciting to be out there," says Freddie. "Bob might have played a little better, but he was never nervous. He's just not the up-and-down type. Like I say, his scores could have been a little lower, but then you can't expect to come up in clover every time."

As the welcome mat back in Azle says: Sometimes you step in it, sometimes you don't.

PUTTING ON THE FLY

IPIALES, COLUMBIA

At this juncture, it might be instructive to tell the story of how golf saved my life.

I was traveling the Andes on the cheap, working off the last of my young man's anomie, when I briefly became very interested in the high-altitude, high anxiety sport of South American bus racing—a pastime that three decades later remains pretty much unchanged, which is to say, as bone-chilling as an Incan blood ritual.

I was, I admit, something of a poker player in those days, but it wasn't gambler's adrenaline that got me on the Ecuador-or-bust local that night. You can't make a peso betting on your own survival in South America; there's not an OTB to be found on the entire continent. No, I was only on the bus because I was so broke I would have stolen flies from a blind tarantula.

As a kid, I'd always read the box scores of South American bus plunges, following the thing in an off-hand way, like a baseball fan in a town without baseball. I knew all the major crashes and mortality rates. There were 22 fewer Peruvians on Christmas Eve in 1962 after a bus made a left-hand turn on a right-hand cliff. The 1971 season hit rock bottom when a rookie Chilean driver and his 46 fares overslid the bag on a mountain road at Puyehe, near the Argentine border. But the disaster by which all others are measured occurred in 1972, when an old Greyhound bus rolled down a ravine near Ayacucho, killing all 44 Peruvians on board. "Another one bites the dust," observed Ximena, my Peruvian girlfriend at the time. She had grown up in the grinding poverty of Cuzco, where bus disasters were no big deal. To my constant amazement (and sometimes horror), she and her relatives were even more insouciant about bus crashes than me.

I was, as I say, merely a casual aficionado of death by falling bus until personal experience took me over the median strip of comfortable contemplation. On that fateful day I was in a Colombian bus, jostling along the knobby spine of the Andes, on my (roundabout) way to visit Ximena's parents. The *South American Handbook* informed me that "bus travel in Colombia is far from dull ... Breakdowns are many. It is not for weak hearts, queasy stomachs, or long legs." Or those, I might add, hoping to live to see 30.

It was, I recall, a particularly bilious evening when I boarded the bus in Ipiales, bound for Quito, Ecuador, a seven-hour journey that's 350 miles as the crows fly, if there were any. I found myself in the midst of a litter of kittens, a parrot, two sheep, half a dozen chickens, and 60 Ecuadorians of various shapes and intentions, all packed in as densely as the Marx Brothers in Groucho's stateroom. This was not the Old Patagonian; it was, rather, the Disorient Express. To distract myself from mounting anxiety, I began flipping through the handbook. "Try roast guinea pig on Wednesday," it advised.

I was seated behind the driver, or, I should say, wedged against him by a sack of coconuts owned by a beet-nosed prostitute. She was indefatigably talkative, and, in her spider-web miniskirt, dressed for the morning social at the House of All Nations in Bogota. Our driver was no less a striking figure—enormous and unbathed, an anaconda tattoo coiling and uncoiling on his bicep.

Beet Nose began yammering into his ear the instant we pulled out.

Ignoring her, he steered with his right hand and wiped the windshield with his left elbow, playing bumper tag with the bus in front of us—all the while jerking away from the edge of an 8,000-foot precipice with prescient tugs on the wheel. The several buses behind us screamed to keep up.

Racing is serious business for South American busdrivers. Whoever gets to the poorly marked stops first collects the passengers and their money (often, the equivalent of about 2 or 3 cents). The competition is made all the more dicey because the buses are never inspected, rarely come in for major maintenance, and routinely ride on tires as bald as a Boy Scout's knee. Persevering through all this, Pan-American drivers earn great, if short-lived, reputations. Ours was a bona fide star. He steered, it seemed, by sonar, somehow making one hairpin (and hair-raising) curve after another. He could barely see the road for the decals festooned all over the windshield, images of the bus driver's Holy Trinity—the Virgin Mary, Che Guevara, and Mickey Mouse.

On one of the rare straightaways, I turned and took in my fellow passengers. Most, I knew, were Ecuadorian smugglers, returning home with trunk loads of duty-free goods bought in Bogota. In the back of the bus, a jangling kid was crying. He was three feet high and maybe four feet wide. Whenever a customs agent boarded the bus at a pit stop, the boy would collapse on the floor with a loud clank. His illness, I soon discerned, was caused by an excess of pots and pans tucked under his belt.

Beet Nose had long since filled my shirt with post-Colombia artifacts: silverware, tuna fish cans, Flintstone jelly glasses. I sat rather stiffly. I had to. The vintage putters she shoved down my back—Burke Ding-A-Lings—acted as a kind of back brace. The police didn't think to search me, assuming, apparently, that lumpy-shirted gringos were too faint of heart to be smugglers.

On a dead uphill stretch, our gears grinding to make the grade, our driver squeezed a cabbie against the side of a tunnel. The cabbie roared up on our left flank yelling

"Assassin," playing cat and mouse with us at 9,000 feet. Skidding around curves, purblind in the pitch dark, we overtook two buses and bolted through the town of Ibarra. Like a 747 pilot minimizing turbulence, our driver assured us that no more than two wheels were ever over the edge.

It didn't put me at ease, though, when we screamed up behind a battered yellow school bus and tried to pass it on the outside. In this case, the outside was seemingly six inches wide and definitely 9,343 feet down. Portions of the road crumbled under our wheels, and for what may have been the first time in the history of South American bus transportation, a driver hit the brakes. Fortunately, the driver in question was ours. But in the next breath he downshifted—*screeeeech*—and the gearshift broke off in his hand. He snarled and waved it uselessly overhead.

I started frantically searching my shirt, hoping that besides the dry goods and pottery, Beet Nose had thought to stuff a parachute there as well. Instead, I drew forth one one of Burke's Ding-A-Lings. Without so much as blinking, Beet Nose grabbed the putter from me and handed it to the driver. On the fly, he jammed it into a hole in the floor, and kicked the seizing engine into fifth. We made the last turn with a good inch-and-a-half to spare, and roared into Quito behind the school bus, a respectable second.

As Beet Nose, the bus driver, the parrot, the chickens, the sheep, and the jangly kid calmly disembarked, I remained in my seat, mouth agape. *Had this really happened? Was this all a dream? Am I ... alive?* I was still seated a half-hour later when the bus started reboarding. As I scurried off the bus, I resolved to hitchhike from here on.

But it wasn't until a week later that I finally swore off bus racing. I'd bought a bus ticket to Cuzco and boarded in Ayacucho.

Inexplicably, I had the bus to myself.

A gaucho in a poncho came on and explained, "Gringo, this bus *malo*."

"What do you mean, *malo*?"

It was the third anniversary of *El Dia de la Pena del Galgo Majado* (The Day of the Sorrow of the Mashed Greyhound). Same day, same line, and, for all I knew, the same bus, resurrected for one last run. "On this day, gringo, no one rides the bus."

Neither did I. It was Wednesday, so I went to a cafe and had the roast guinea pig.

FLAKING OUT

TOCO, TEXAS

Rocky Thompson arches his thick, evangelistic eyebrows and denies he's a flake. Back home in Toco, Texas—where he's the mayor—flakes are unreliable, irresponsible, downright reprehensible. "In short, jerks," Hizzoner says in a voice as sharp as freshly sliced jalapeno peppers. "Like in that movie *Thelma & Louise.*"

In that movie, he tells you, "Louise, or maybe Thelma, blows a guy away. She wants to lay low in Mexico, but Thelma, or maybe Louise, gets antsy and wants to surrender to the police." Whereupon Louise—Thelma?—says, "Don't flake out on me."

"Meaning, don't be a jerk," explains Thompson. "So please, don't call me a flake, even if you mean wild and crazy, which I certainly am. Because where I'm from, a flake is a jerk, and while I might be a jerk, I'm not unreliable."

Thompson was flouting flakery one January day at the Infiniti Tournament of Champions in Carlsbad, California. "I've wanted to play here ever since I entered my very first pro tournament, the 1964 Indy 500 Classic," Thompson said. "Of course in those days I didn't drive the Rockmobile." It wasn't until 1966 that fellow pro Bob Goalby told him, "Rocky, if a man's gonna drive the Tour, he's gotta drive it in style." The very next day Thompson dumped his Oldsmobile and bought himself a red Coupe de Ville—the Rockmobile. He has driven various versions of the Rockmobile ever since.

Even with his new wheels, Thompson just couldn't seem to find his way from Indianapolis to the winner's circle: The trip took him through Venezuela, Panama, Australia, and New Zealand; from the Indian Open in New Delhi to the Bucaramanga Open in Colombia to the Space Coast Open in Titusville, Florida; and to many other satellite sites too obscure to mention. "I've played in places where there isn't even a town," he says. And the trek lasted 27 years.

In nearly three decades on the PGA Tour, Thompson, the son of a Texas oilman who long financed his career, earned just $141,096 and failed to win a single tournament. "I don't think I could have gone 27 years without a victory," says Chi Chi Rodriguez. "My clothes would have gone out of style."

King Rabbit, they called Thompson, because his brows were carrot-colored and he hopped from tournament to tournament, trying to qualify and to pick up a little lettuce. Nobody ever played in more Tour events without an exemption. "I wonder how I made it through all those Monday qualifiers," he muses. "Just try playing 600 Tour events fighting the 36-hole cut, knowing if you don't make it, you're not going to get a dime."

Thompson drifted in links limbo, just above the family safety net, until joining the Senior Tour in the fall of 1989. "Suddenly, I hit pay dirt," Thompson says. He made $308,915 in 1990, another $435,794 in 1991. And—wonder of wonders —Thompson actually won a tournament. Two of them, in fact: the MONY Syracuse Senior Classic and the Digital Seniors Classic in Concord, Massachusetts. The Syracuse victory snapped his winless streak at 611 tournaments and earned him a ticket to Carlsbad. "It feels the same to win on the Senior Tour as it does in the juniors," he says. "Then again, how the hell would I know?"

Thompson can turn a phrase as felicitously as an old cowboy can drop a rope around a mustang's neck. "I may be old in body, but I have a teenager's brain," he says. Who else moonwalks on the putting green ("I like Guy Lombardo, but I love Van Halen")? Or relaxes before rounds by staring into a blinking light-and-sound gizmo he calls Mo Chine? Or performs what appear to be sexual calisthenics after sinking a 40-footer? Or carries a low-tech putter that looks like a ski pole jammed into a coconut Frozfruit? Or fears the Putt Fairy?

Before 1991 the closest Thompson had come to winning a tournament was 25 years prior at the Azalea Open in Wilmington, North Carolina. He would have forced a sudden-death playoff that day if his putt at 18 hadn't died a half-inch from the cup. "A victory there would have changed my first-day pairings forever," he reflects. "Never again would I have been required to tee off at 7 a.m., when the greens are frosty, or at 3:15 in the afternoon, when they've been torn up by spikes."

He pulls in a long breath.

"Another half an inch, and my whole life might have changed."

Another breath.

"Who knows, I might not be mayor of Toco."

Toco (pop. 164) squats in the middle of the Great Nothing, a bleached expanse of Southwestern landscape. "Toco's just a little deal west of Paris," Thompson says. And he doesn't mean the one where Jerry Lewis is considered a *genie comique.*

The town consists of 38 homes, three water tanks and a liquor store that doubles as the jail. No prisoners have been taken since 1972, when a band of desperadoes were locked up for drinking, handily enough, in the store's parking lot. Mayor Bill Thompson, Rocky's father, allowed himself a few liberties with his office. "My father held court for all 15 of them dudes," Rocky says. "He appointed himself judge of the Toco Territory."

When Bill died, in 1983, Rocky took over as mayor. He has been reelected and reelected and reelected. "Has anyone ever run against me?" he says, incredulously. "Who the hell would want to?" His municipal duties run from impounding stray dogs to unclogging sewer lines. Once a year he shows up in Paris to host the Rocky Thompson Shootout, a sort of free-for-all in which duffers are blasted with water pistols as beer is poured on their Titleists. "The idea is to screw up the other players' shots without touching them or impairing the flight of the ball," Thompson says. Foghorns are legal, even encouraged. But firecrackers had to be outlawed in 1986 after a Roman candle sparked a fire in an adjoining field. "Just about anything goes in the Shootout," Thompson says. "It's what golf might have been like in the Old West."

For Rocky, the Old West is romantically real. He grew up singing "Pistol Packin' Mama," "Don't Fence Me In," and "The Yellow Rose of Texas." He believed in cowboys and Indians, in Tom Mix and in the Lone Ranger, Gene Autry, and Roy Rogers, Johnny Mack Brown and Red Ryder. Thompson took his name from Alan Rocky Lane, a Saturday-afternoon-serial cowpoke from Thompson's youth who "whupped up on the bad guys and never failed."

Thompson was born in Shreveport, Louisiana. When he was 4, his family moved to Wichita Falls, Texas. His father later started the Thompson Oil Company, from which Toco took its name. "I'm not a bit sorry or apologetic that when I was born, my daddy was rich," Rocky says.

When Rocky was 12, his old man signed him up for golf lessons at the Wichita Falls Country Club. Within two years Rocky was shooting par. At 16 he averaged 68. "I had the world's greatest short game," he says. At 17 he saw his game balloon to an average of 73. "I had the world's worst long game." In 1956 he was paired with a Canadian slugger named Gary Cowan at the Jaycee junior championship in Fargo, North Dakota. Off the final tee Cowan outhit him by 50 yards. "I decided that if I could drive the ball farther, no one on the planet could beat me," Thompson says.

Thompson's remodeled swing looked like the swing of another Rocky—Colavito. "I traded my smooth, Gene Littler deal for a lashing, gashing piece of junk," he says. Fifty-two years later he's still trying to regain his graceful stroke.

He often partied harder than he practiced. "The first 10 years on the Tour, I was a bachelor," he recalls. "I loved to dance. Most nights I was out late doing the twist, the Watusi, the James Brown. The women got me. No question, the women got me. Then I got married, and my wife got me. I didn't get totally serious about golf until I was 49."

With his 50th birthday approaching, Thompson spent all of 1989 prepping for the Senior PGA Qualifying School tournament. All, that is, but three days. "I wanted to beat balls on those days, too," he says. "But my wife kept me too busy with the honey-do's."

Meaning what?

"You know, Honey, do this. Honey, do that."

In the tournament, about 450 people competed for eight Tour exemptions. Thompson led the field with an opening-day 67, followed by scores of 72, 71, and 71. He won the event by a record 10 strokes.

Thompson still goes to great lengths to win: 50 inches,

to be exact. That's the size of Big Red, the driver that helped him place third in the 1991 seniors driving competition. Once a singles hitter, Thompson has become a real long-ball threat. That, combined with his soft touch—his short game was one of the best on the Senior Tour.

Oddly, Thompson uses several different putters. When one fails him, he switches to another—often on the same hole. "If a putter does well," he says, "I reward it by letting it play the next hole."

Does Thompson think his putters have minds of their own? "A flake would probably say yes, but I don't believe they do," he says. "At least not yet."

They do, nonetheless, have distinct personalities. Two of them come in the black-and-silver color scheme of the Oakland Raiders: what he calls the 650 (because it cost $650) and Faded Jake, whose black paint is beginning to— sorry, Rocky—flake off. The other putter is the oddly angled Low Rider, a homemade number that seems ideal for performing root canal work on a hippopotamus. To wield it, Thompson must assume a catcher's crouch, plant his elbows on his knees and punch the ball toward the hole. If the putt falls in, he shouts, "Low Rider! Low Rider! Lowwwwwwww Rider!" If it doesn't, he blames the Putt Fairy.

A cruel and vengeful creature, the Putt Fairy, says Thompson, "punishes those who don't keep their mouths off the putt." A remark as innocent as "It's in!" will cause her to nudge a ball toward an unnatural break. "Sometimes the Putt Fairy gets so offended, she'll jerk that sucker out of that hole!" he says. "Of course, you know she's the wife of Satan."

Of all golf's gremlins, Thompson considers the Phantom to be the most fiendish. "He decides whether you'll get good or bad kicks," Thompson says. He calls good kicks Nicklauses; bad ones are Thompsons. "Sometimes the Phantom likes me and gives me a Nicklaus," says Thompson. "But Nicklaus never gets a Thompson. Never."

Thompson got Thompsoned during his rookie seniors season at the Vantage in San Antonio. Going into the final hole, he was a stroke ahead of Lee Trevino. But his drive found a sprinkler head, kicked dead left, and landed behind a tree. Thompson chipped out and wound up with a bogey. Trevino eagled the par-5 hole and won the title.

Thompson finally got Nicklaused three months later at the MONY Classic, where he and Jim Dent were tied for the lead after 17 holes on the final day. On 18, Thompson hooked his tee shot into the rough and behind a weeping willow. Ignoring the obvious irony of the ball's resting place, he somehow slinked a 6-iron to within 14 feet of the flag. Dent was long, 35 feet away. Thompson two-putted. When Dent muffed what would have been a score-tying six-footer, Thompson was suddenly a champion. He executed a hip-jiggle, then thrust his fist into the air like a down-home revolutionary.

Afterward, Thompson said, "I've been playing 27 years. My goal was to win a tournament. Just one week I wanted to be The Man. Until this week, as best I can count, I was oh-for-611. But now, if I never win again ... right now ... this minute, today, this week, I am The Man!" So loud did he scream those last four words as he stood near the green that he lost his voice for a week. He was hoarse again in September when he won the Digital Seniors. This time he celebrated with a vaguely erotic variation on the push-and-pull. "I am The Man!" he exulted once again. "I am The Man!"

Still, Thompson got little recognition. He spent so long in the shadows that even some seniors didn't know who he was. At the 1991 Tournament of Champions awards banquet, Calvin Peete introduced him as Rocky Thomas. "You know what I should have done?" Thomas told a clump of fellow senior citizens in the locker room the following day. "I should have shouted, 'Stop! Stop this program!' "

"Then I should have said, 'I started in '64. I finally get a chance to play on the Senior Tour, but I have to qualify. I hit one million, two hundred thousand practice balls and win one of eight qualifying spots. I finally win my first tournament. Now I'm to be announced to come up onstage to get a medal, and I'm introduced as Rocky Thomas.' "

He fused his carroty brows until they formed a single smudge across his forehead. " 'If I'm going to bust my buns for 27 years and go through all the heartache and pain and aggravation, I at least want everybody in this room, including Rodney Peete, to know that my name is Rocky Thompson. Thompson! Thank you.' "

The seniors laughed uproariously and broke into prolonged applause.

Thompson's smile was pert, twisted. "People think I'm nuts, but I don't care," he said. "The truth is, I am nuts." He paused, then added, "But I am not a flake."

LORD LOVE A BLIMP

MILWAUKEE, WISCONSIN

There's something lovable about the Goodyear blimp. It's big and round and looks soft and cuddly. When it passes overhead at golf tournaments it draws men, women, children, and dogs out of their houses. They look up in wonder and adoration. How could anyone not love a blimp? Somebody once took a potshot at one of the Goodyears floating over the Greater Milwaukee Open, igniting commentator Paul Harvey to rage, "What are we coming to? They're even shooting at the blimp!"

"The blimp is positive," says Mickey Wittman. "It stands for everything that's good in this country." Wittman is Blimpman. In the late 1960s he was an advance man for the blimp, phoning up newspapers and radio and TV stations to tell them the blimp is coming, the blimp is coming! Now, as

Goodyear's manager of broadcasting, he helps set up blimp routes and acts as a liaison with the networks. Wittman probably attends more pro and amateur golf events than anyone, but he usually watches them from a TV truck.

Largely through Wittman's efforts, the Goodyear blimp coverage has ballooned from 16 to 65 sports events a year on national TV. The blimps used to show up only at the Grand Slams. Now you see them at everything from Q-School qualifiers to the Fort Linda, Montana Scramble.

Goodyear has three blimps—each with a crew of three—that wander over the United States: *Enterprise* (based in Pompano Beach, Florida), *America* (based in Houston) and *Columbia* (based in Los Angeles). Until the late 1980s, the only other blimp in the world in regular operation toured Europe for Goodyear.

Wittman is the guy people call when they get a promotional brainstorm and need a blimp to blanket Keokuk, Iowa, with circulars or to buzz their daughter's Sweet 16 party in Bryn Mawr, Pennsylvania. But the blimp schedules are so packed with sporting events, it's hard to reserve a date. Still, the blimps have had time to search for the Loch Ness monster, track whales in the North Atlantic, and help capture the dreaded Jack the Reaper, a naked fugitive loose in a Kansas cornfield.

For a blimpman, Wittman is pretty lean and rangy. He used to play basketball, though you'd hardly know it from the places he performed. In college, he played for two schools that no longer have basketball programs. His semi-pro teams, the Goodyear Wayfoots and the Phillips 66ers of the National Industrial Basketball League, aren't around anymore, either. Even the pro teams that drafted him—the St. Louis Hawks of the NBA and the Anaheim Amigos of the ABA—went kaput. "Working with the blimp," he says, "is the only thing I've ever done that had any lasting merit."

Blimps seem to bring out the little kid in people. Even hard-nosed network producers melt at the thought of the blimp. "Hello, Blimpie," one shouted off-camera during a recent telecast from Yankee Stadium. "Oh, Blimpie, oh, Blimpie Blimpie. Mickey, I forgot my glasses. Can you send the blimp over to my home in Jersey and have it lower a rope?"

Wittman is so wrapped up in blimpdom that he thinks of his second marriage in blimp time. "I met my wife, Barbra, before a Monday Night Football game," he says. "The Bears vs. the Rams. We bought the license at the Indy 500, got hitched between a Braves game and the All-Star Game, and returned from the honeymoon in time for a golf tournament in Virginia."

He talks about the blimps as if they were alive. The original *America* once smashed against its hangar in Houston during a high wind. Its body was punctured and helium seeped out. "She whined like a dying animal, a dinosaur," Wittman says. "She made such a sad sound that I had to cry. It was very traumatic." The airship had to be decommissioned. Mourners sent flowers.

The blimps have been used mostly for what are called beauty shots: skylines, sunsets and the like. But occasionally, they get into the action. Wittman gushes over a remote-control eve-in-the-sky camera that can isolate particular golfers and their swings, and use the shots as a kind of electronic instructional video. But the first time he tried it out during a satellite tournament, the golfers looked like lima beans floating in a murky broth. Wittman blames poor lighting for that failure. "The camera," he says, "represents the future of blimp camera work."

Wittman is actually doing his second stint as Blimp-man. He quit blimping back in 1975. "After seven years, I had blimp burnout," he says. "I OD'd on helium." For three years he tried other things, including going to shopping-center school. "But everyone who leaves the blimp has to come back," he says. "I mean, where else can grown men get paid for playing with balloons?"

THE ROCKET CART@

LANDENBERG, PENNSYLVANIA

From: Godwin John
Subject: PRIVATE!!
UNITED BANK FOR AFRICA PLC, LAGOS NIGERIA.
Attn: Ogar Lidz,

My name is Godwin John , the Western District Manager of
United Bank forAfrica Plc. (UBA). There is a domiciliary
account opened in this bank in September 1980, in the
name of Mr. Charles B. Smith, an expatriate who then was
the manager of Petroleum & Technical Support services.
The account was operated for about 1 year and 6 months
after/whiich,, it became dormant forabout 81/2 years. Mr.
Smith died in June 1990 in an crash on a golf course. After
going through some old files, I observed that the account

owner's next of kin is his wife who died with him in the golf cart crash. This has then made it impossible for anyone to lay claims to the funds deposited in the account. The top echelons of the bank are also unaware of the details of this account because of, its,,, length of dormancy. The amount left in the account is US $18,372,000.00. I have observed that if I do not transfer this money out of the country, it would be forfeited. I therefore want to transfer this money into a foreign account of an Individual or corporate body for safekeeping and investments. Since the funds belongs to a foreigner, it is then necessary that only a foreigner can lay claims to it, this is where your co-operation and partnership is needed.And with my position and knowledge of the history of the account, the transaction would be a huge success. I propose a meeting between us as soon as you indicate your willingness to co-operate with me in this transaction and a sharing formula of 80% for me and 20% for you at the end of the transaction. The transfer of the money to your mandated account will be by swift to reach your bank within 24 hours.

I look forward to your response by e-mail and also include your private telephone and fax numbers for more confidential discussions, I will want us to conclude this transaction on or before next week. Yours faithfully,

Mr.Godwin John

Dear faithful Godwin,
Woah Nelly! This sounds like the deal I've been waiting for. can't believe my luck and I sure could use the swag. tell me

more. Your bud. Ogar,
* P.S. I love golf too*

My Dear Ogar,

I thank you very much for your response to my proposal. I sorry for the late response to your reply, I am just coming back from calabar state, I went for an officials duty. I will want us to discuss on phone regarding this

transaction which will be of a great benefit to us in future. Already, I have started all arrangement regarding the transfer. I will want you to call me today on my personal phone number : 00234-803-3217481.

Hoping to hear from you soonest. Your brother/partner, Godwin.

Dear partner of faithful brother and buddy Godwin,
You are the best! I'm been wondering how I'll ever get out from this little jam that I found myself and you are the ticket as we say and, answer to my fondest and most spiritual of pra,yers and such. I have, so many questions whose ,answers I should know from you and the like. This poor and dead Mr. Charles Smith. What was his handicap, his score at the time of the cart mishap and make/model was he driving? was he wearing a seat belt. In some states here it is THE LAW. Buckle up for safety, we say. I do not like the rules of my society that well but ones like BUCKLE UP is fine as well as dandy with a hacker such as me. Does Chuck's wife not entitle her,self to the golf death money that it hers,, so rightfully, I would prseume by the accident/death/golf laws

governing Lagos? Or does she not wish to take the money tainted perhaps by the death of her dear and ,beloved? Philosophical I am by nature and also trusting who believes the All/mighty has graced you upon me for our mutual and everlasting benefit but these questions are ones my wife Leashon who I tell you lacks my humanity and does not always respect my dreams wants me to ask of you which i do not know why. exactly. Your partner in sincerity as well as fondness and humanity. Ogar

P.s. calabar state – cool!!!

My Dear brother Ogar,

I thank you very much for your urgent response to my mail of this afternoon. I appreciate your questions as well, that shows that you are careful personal which is required in this type of transaction. Be informed that Mr Smith died on the course with his wife who is suppose to be the next of kin to her husband, and there is no record of any of mr Smith's relation that has shown any interest regarding the claim. I want you to know that all arrangement regarding the transaction has been worked out before now, and I want to also let you know that this transaction is risk-free, all I need from you is cooperation/trust. And i want to be sure that my funds will be safe in your care after the transfer. As soon as we take possession of the funds, I will collect all the whole document from my bank and distroy them before coming over to meet with you for our investment project.You have to also remember that I have told them that you contacted me to assist you, so I am your local representative, that is what i told them at the bank. I will want you to call me this night or tomorrow morning so that we can discuss some vital things reg,ard,ing this transaction. It is very important we discuss, to enable me notify you of the things i did to/day regarding the transfer of the funds. meanwhile, I will want you to send your account information where the whole funds will be transferred. Remember that we can not claim the funds until you open an account with our bank. These are the things I will want us to discuss on phone. Already, the amount our bank is demending for the domiciliay account is in my personal account, I will have to change the money from nigeria curency (naria)to US$ tomorrow, that is why I want us to talk before I proceed.

I am anxiously waiting to hear from you.
Thank you once again for your urgent response.
Your brother/partner,
Godwin.

Dear brother of partners in filial fondness,
Thank you for explaining so much of which I did not know and hoped to ask but which by I was unaware to ,even dream that you would tell me. In my last letter did I inform you of Leashon my wife? She says ask Godwin the questions becaus,e no one will give you that golf loot of such magnitude just to have a bank account. Ha I say. Just w,ait because Godwin is a good man and works in a bank and is one of the most respectful men in Nigeria,. Anyway I, had a ques-

tion of my own that Leashon do not even think of. It is about Chuck B. Smith, the accident victi,m of death by cart. In grade school I knew a Chuck Smith whose middle name I cannot remember but Bernard is maybe the one. His sisters name was Unique. Î remember this because I always said Oh what a uniqu,e name and she woul;d laugh big from the belly, not that her belly was big although perhaps it was but I cannot remember correctly. Anyway, Chuck moved away from my neighborhood in 4th grade. Could he have com,e to Lagos and made the loot of many millions and then become killed, in the cart without his belt. This questio,n haunted my sleep last night and now I must ask. Truly and in wonderful brotherhood of partner unions. Ogar.

Dear Dear Brother Ogar,
I thank you for all your words. But, you must be very serious regarding the things I told you yesterday. I am hoping to hear from you. Thanks for your cooperation. Your brother/partner, Godwin.

My dear, dear, dear Godwin,
This is the greatest and dearest news of all. Your generosity is the talk of my community froim which I dwell and live my life, also eat. Everyone here now praises your name and your deeds, as well. The poor misfortune, of the man who died in the golf cart and his wife yes has turned into a great FORTUNE for those of us without who lack the resources of, he who has passed and they being, dead who have none. The beauty part of this heavensent and earthlybound gift is

that so many of the things I had hoped and once if, not wished for can now had the chance of fruition and wholesome oneedness. For instance, Godwin my brother — actually my half-brother because it is a mother and not a father who is not the same that we share — Edgar, whose teeth need the fix as the protrusion from his mouth makes even the grapes difficult to eat from where he stands, has an idea of genius of which the world cannot wait but now funding he can find! It is called a rocket golf cart and modern it is because it runs not on electricity but on corn and not on corn oil but CORN COBS! I don't know if in Lagos you have a machine called a JUICER but here we do and this ROCKET CART@ of Edgar's design runs much the same way in that you plunge the corncob into the ROCKET GEARS and I don't know how science works but the car moves, Godwin, it moves! No scientist not even Einstein or such as him has even dreamed of a machine like this. Edgar needs but $7 million to see his dream/reality and I intend to help him some if not all, much. If you put some of your own wealth in Edgar's ROCKET CART@, like corncobs into the gears, (I say more than a few million, dollars or Nigerian currency will do) we can sell the cart in india, a dear country which has hundreds of golfers and golf course. many indian golfers would love such a machine to, soar above the fairways and clouds. With the money we make, we can set up a ROCKET CART@ business in china, which has many golfers more and chances to make many more millions of dollars or if your prefer Nigerian currency. I cannot wait for all this to transpire, Godwin. We will be be very rich indeed. And what a fit-

ting testament to golfer Chuck Smith and his equally dead wife! Please let me know what you think. Your dearest of brother partners. Ogar

Dear Partner Ogar,
Again, your words are interesting and I am still hoping to hear from you. We will speak of many serious things, your brother's rocket cart being one. My bank has several questions. It is urgent that I talk to you at once. I am waiting for you to call. Your brother, Godwin.

My dearest brother of partners Godwin,
More fantasic news: My brother Edgar has agreed to give us the patent, for his new ROCKET CART@! Is this fantastic or what? We will be able to sell it in Burma and Sri Lanka and almost all of, Southeast Asia! We will soon be, billionaires with 10s of thousands of dollars, I assure you. Edgar merely requires, a small, a very very small I promise you, downpayment and it will ALL BE Ours. The dreams of you and I will become truth, my brother and partner, oh yes they will, surely so and always.

How shall we arrange to transfer the, funds? You mention a small complication with the banking, laws of your homeland. Will this be a difficulty? Surely you can convince the wise bankers of Lagos to help fund what must, obviously be the first great invention of the new century. perhaps they would care to invest as well. Oh what a wondrous day this surely truly is, Godwin. We will be rich beyond our wilder dreams.

With great friendship and honor and brotherly partner-
ship, I remain. Ogar.

Dear Ogar my friend and brother,
It is time to stop the words. You must call immediately me
on my personal phone number : 00234-803-3217481. Ever
faithfully,
  Godwin.

My dear excellent Godwin,
I have been trying desperately to, reach you by the mobile
telephone of yours to discuss our banking transaction and
my, other brother's ROCKET CART@ invention and numer-
ous other things but the number you have given me does not
seem to be working to my answering, satisfaction. Does it
require some numismatic prefixture to which I am unaware
or not comprehending? Please, answer me quickly, Godwin
my brother/partner as we have much, much to discuss and
plan for our future together in the business world of golf and
life. Have you given much, thought what as to, we shall, call
our company? I was thinking perhaps "Godgar" or "Odwin"
to show the world our union as people of two continents
brought together for the good, of humanity and golf and
such. have you an opinion yourself of your own making
and thought? I look forward to answers to these multiple
and numerous questions. With much, brotherly and part-
nerly love in kinship and friendship and golfship and world-
ship. Ogar

My Dear Brother Ogar,

I am very sorry for the late response to your mail. I've not been arround since friday. Meanwhile I have reconfirm my number to you. I want to let you know that everything regarding this transaction is in order, please I want you to be very serious regarding this transaction, I will also need to talk with you on phone before the end of tomorrow, because the approval

regarding the transfer might be out tomorrow, so I will need us discuss some vital things. Be also informed that our bank policy stated that as

the next of kin to Mr. Charles Smith, I am already making arrangement for all these things which is cost me alot of money. I want you to understand my mean objective regarding my part of share, to invest with you in the area of investment that will be of a great benefit to us in future. Kindly call me as soon as you receive this mail. Please informed that some time our telecommunication system is very defficult to get, but keep trying you must deffinately get through. Thank you for your cooperation/effort. Your brother/partner, Godwin.

Dearest brother of partner brothers Godwin,
The money is so close to being ours that I can taste it with my hands, Godwin, taste it with the fingers of my very hands that swings my 3-wood and types the letters which you read so thoughtfully. But it is so frustrating! Every time I try to call you night and day and morning even I cannot get through. What Have I done to deserve this? The fingers

*of my moneytasting 3-wood hands are ready to GRASP the
fruit of our business/dealings and yet I cannot reach you.
The sweat, it pours from my furry/brow. My brother Edgar
has his own deadline for us and it is less than 48 hours
away — that is just 4 days from now! What shall we do? i
cannot reach, you by money/hands or phone and I fear the,
wondrous ROCKET CART@ may be slipping away from us.
Tell me Godwin, is there some other way of communicating
with you, in the dear excel;lent country of Nigeria? there
must be, Godwin, there simply must. be. It's is God's will to
see the untold riches of our new multi/national company
Godgar or if you will Odwin, though I believe I prefer the
first, I don't know you decide. Do you have a ham/radio or
perhaps does some trucker you know? I am no scientist as
I have told you ,but I think fate has bonded by some kind of
cosmic epoxy, Godwin. Please help me and instruct me on
what to do. Fondly and sincere earnest/brotherhood and
such. Ogar.*

My Dear Brother Ogar,

I thank you very much for your urgent response to my
mail. I am very happy to receive your regarding this transaction which will be of a great benefit to our families in future. Like I informed you in my proposal to you regarding
the funds, the funds is real, and I need your support and
assist to move this funds out of my bank. that is the only
assistance I need from you. Please call today. My Number
is +234 803 3217481. Your Partner and brother, Godwin

*Dearest of Sincere and Earnest Partner Brothers Godwin,
I have found a solution to our communication problem. We
shall talk by video phone! Near my home is the world famous Nortell Laboratories where wondrous wonders of science that even Einstein would not have envisioned are
invention/fruition. I do not know if Nigeria has its video
phones in place but why not wire me $100,000 a small and
meager sum in regard to the Sultan's Treasure we are about
to see and I will buy two world and international Nortell
video phones for our usage and business transaction talking pleasure? It is but a short distance from my home off the
sixth green or what was once my home because these recent
business/dealings have so changed my life that I no longer
live in the old domicile that once sheltered me. My wife
Leashon calls me a fool for my dreaming (she says "The
funds is NOT real!") and my children they spit upon me and
call me a fool too. I say hell with you and leave (I do not
mean you, dear Godwin, who is my brother and friend and
partner in all earnestness and goodwill and global sincerity.
It is they my wretched family who do are infidels and unbe-
lievers and tell me never to come back). As we know (ha!) I
will get the, last and final laugh. They have the car and the
home and such, but I have the BANK ACCOUNT in ,which,
you will transfer the, dead Mr. Chuck B. Smiths money and
we shall berich ourselves and play golf for the rest of our
lives. So Leashon is the fool, no? When I ride around the
courses of the world in my solid gold rocket cart@ she will
be the one to stare in wondrous wonder and cry Oh Og,ar
I've made a mistaken and you really hav,e the untold riches*

that you claimed and you and Godwin are great/powerful-businessmen, who will soon fill the streets and air and the golf paths of Sri Lanka and many other countries in Southeast Asia with, ROCKET CARTS@ and such. And I will say Fool on you! You had your chance and you think I the fool. Ha! Now I am the rich one and flying here and there and scoring eight below par, so you keep that house and children I don't need. Godwin my partner/brother , does it get better than this? Ogar.

THE SPACE BETWEEN

FAIRFIELD, IOWA

t's Halloween, and Ed Hipp is surrounded by enough cosmetics to resurrect Norma Desmond from *Sunset Boulevard*. Resplendent in black pumps and a white brocade gown, he outlines his mouth with lipliner and trowels foundation onto his cheeks. Hipp smears on some go-to-hell scarlet lipstick, and his makeup is done. The 44-year-old family man wears a face that has become an odd caricature of womanly beauty. "I'll tell you the difference between our golf team and others in Iowa," he deadpans as he leads his kids away for a little trick-or-treating. "We're the only one with a coach who's a cross-dresser."

That turns out to be the least of the differences. As coach at tiny Maharishi High (enrollment: 179), in Fairfield, Hipp applies mystical precepts to golf. His unorthodox training techniques run from sun salutations to aromatherapy to pulse therapy to a hopped-up form of transcendental meditation called yogic flying. Hipp's Maharishi Pioneers are undeniably transcendent. In 1996, in only their third season, they won the Iowa state high school Class 1A championship by 19 strokes. Hipp called it a "consciousness-based victory."

To clear their heads and calm their nerves, golfers try a host of relaxation strategies. Greg Norman dabbles in Zen; Tiger Woods can be hypnotized when talking to his psychological coach over the phone. Hipp says TM is the only method that both flushes a golfer's mind of thought and joins his consciousness with other invisible fields of the universe, such as gravity. "Having gained equanimity in birdie and bogey, then I am to come out and play," Hipp wrote in his two-act play, *The Song of Golf.* "In this yoga, the resolute intellect is one-pointed, like a wedge shot in a windless place."

At six feet and 185 pounds, Hipp seems to be a solid enough phenomenon. He's a gentle, measured, corduroyed kind of guy who preaches inner peace and metaphysical fitness. His golfers meditate up to three hours a day, eat no red meat, and get to bed by 10 p.m. "Our whole lives are a preshot routine," says Pioneers captain Noah Schechtman. "Ed never puts competing before enlightenment. He's the only golf coach in the state who spends more time coaching the player than the swing."

Duffer dharma is more elusive than a Zen koan. "Golf is a game," offers Hipp's own golfing guru, Fred Shoemaker, who founded the School for Extraordinary Golf in Carmel Valley, California. "In order to have a game, something must be more important than something else. If what already *is* is more important than what *isn't*, game's over. Golf is a game in which what *isn't* is more important than what *is*."

What is certain is that after dropping out of North Carolina State in 1972, Hipp went to Europe, where he learned TM. He liked meditating so much that he began to teach it. In 1981 he moved to Fairfield, where adepts of Maharishi Mahesh Yogi were living and sowing karma amid the corn and bean fields of southern Iowa.

Hipp didn't take up golf until he was 25, but when he did, he took it up devoutly. By 1988 he was managing Fairfield's municipal driving range. It was a marginal operation, and in 1990, Hipp took over the lease. Hipp had his 11-year-old stepson, Devon Abrams, and a bunch of his classmates retrieve range balls. In return they got 50 cents an hour and free lessons. Those early Hippsters became the core of the Maharishi Pioneers. "I taught them to generate each shot from the basis of calmness rather than the basis of reaction," Hipp says. "And that golf is a series of breakdowns. The winner is the one who manages those breakdowns best."

Like Hipp, the Pioneers have more than a little aura of tranquility about them. The coach's most diligent pupil, the aptly named Lyric Duveyoung, used to practice the Bertholy Method of posed positioning for two-and-a-half hours a day. Duveyoung won Fairfield's 1992 junior title as a 14-year-old and has successfully defended it every year since. Three years later he snagged Iowa's Class 1A high school individual crown.

The Pioneers formed in 1994. In their inaugural season, they finished 10-1 in the Southeast Iowa Super Conference and third in the state. In 1995 they were 13-1 and second in the state. The next year they were 13-1 and won it all. Even bad weather doesn't faze them. "The key is patience and surrender," intones Schechtman. "If you get anxious over a bad hole and press, you lose your connection with nature."

To keep that connection, Hipp and his Pioneers meditate twice a day, in the morning and early evening, on sheet-covered mattresses spread out in the Maharishi Patanjali Golden Dome of Pure Knowledge. They practice an advanced form of meditation called TM-Sidhi, otherwise known as yogic flying.

"Golf is a test of mind-and-body coordination," Schechtman says. "Yogic flying is the ultimate test." He folds his legs in a yogic knot, rests his hands lightly in front of him, and silently chants his mantra. For five minutes he idles motionlessly, eyes shut in serene contemplation. Suddenly he begins to shake. And rattle. And roll. And rising to the occasion, he bounces on his bum like a human Super Ball. He hops startlingly high and surprisingly far, propelled, he maintains, only by his belief in the teachings of Maharishi, the Seer of Flying.

Back when spiritual enlightenment could be gauged by the glow on your mood ring, TM consisted of a mantra, a tie-dyed T-shirt, and a mellow vibe. But it's no longer enough to sit around contemplating your navel. Hipp insists you've got to get off your butt if you're going to attain inner peace and save the universe. He claims yogic flying lengthens memory, reduces fatigue, and prolongs youthfulness. But he doesn't stop there. He also maintains that swarms of yogic pilots taking to the air to create a "Unified Field" of consciousness that has made the stock market rise, the crime rate fall, increased the number of patent applications, saved the Florida orange crop, reduced traffic fatalities in Australia and the death toll in Iraq, and influenced Fidel Castro to give up cigars.

According to Maharishi, hopping is only the first stop in the elevator ride to higher awareness. With practice, he says, TMers will reach the second floor, hovering, and eventually free flight. Someday there may be a red-eye to New Delhi. For now, though, everyone but him is too weighed down with stress.

Maharishi Patanjali developed the technique for yogic flying 2,000 years before the Wright Brothers did. But no really serious flying was done by laymen until 1976, when TM founder Maharishi Mahesh Yogi started conducting classes. Now there are more than 100,000 airborne meditators. Still, yogic flying remained as secret as a Captain Midnight decoder ring until Maharishi became concerned with terrorism and world tension. "War is caused by a buildup of stress in the collective consciousness of nations," Hipp explains.

To unclog the collective consciousness and fend off future wars, Maharishi—who died in February 2008 at the age of 91—wanted to form air bases of 7,000 meditators—

the number he divined was needed to achieve world peace. Maharishi arrived at the figure scientifically: He took the square root of 1% of the world's population. Maharishi tried to validate his mystical claims with modern science. Adepts bombard you with testimonials by science faculty, reams of Maharishi International University-commissioned surveys, and topographical brain maps. Hipp maintains that yogic flying defies Newton's laws of gravity and Einstein's theory of relativity and conforms only to the mysterious unified field. "When I'm in the air, I feel like I'm getting a zap of bliss," he says. "Or hitting a really good tee shot, a perfect shot."

Cynicism about all this bliss-zapping circulates among Hipp's fellow coaches. They smelled a rat in Hipp's use of aromatherapy. Maharishi promoted a line of fragrant, mood-altering remedies made from the oil of such herbs as rose, sandalwood, and jasmine. Hipp would give each of the Pioneers an oil-soaked cotton ball. When stressed or nervous, they would pull the balls out of their pockets and take a whiff. During the 1994 state sectionals, a rival coach asked Hipp, "What are your guys smelling?"

"Vata oil."

"Is that a performance enhancer?"

"Yeah, but it's completely natural. It's made from flowers."

The coach protested to the Iowa Athletic Association, which found Maharishi's flower power to be pungent but legal. Since then Hipp has had his Pioneers dab the unguents directly onto their shirts. In one match, a golfer lined up a putt, sniffed one shoulder, eyed the lie, stepped back, and then sniffed his other shoulder. "I always know it's a tough shot when it's a double smell," Hipp says.

Maharishi is part of Maharishi International University, whose campus gives new meaning to the term Peter Pan complex. When you arrive, a team of beaming administrators takes you on a tour. Besides beatific expressions, they wear modest lamb's-wool vests, correct tweed jackets, prudent white shirts, and sincere striped ties. They offer you a Utopian hero sandwich—sprouts and three heavenly cheeses—and lead you through the Reversal of Aging Laboratory and into the Maharishi School of the Age of Enlightenment, where freshly scrubbed girls ages 5 through 18 wear identical white blouses, blue frocks, and red bows; and boys don white shirts, blue sweaters, and red ties. The curriculum covers the three R's as well as the three I's (infinite dynamism, infinite silence, and infinite organizing power).

Next stop is the Maharishi Patanjali Golden Dome of Pure Knowledge, where the silence is broken only by the sound of one man hopping. Legs tightly folded in a yogic knot, hands resting lightly in front of him, one of Hipp's young golfers flops over the spongy mats and onto a stack of mattresses. "Going up feels completely natural," he says. "The surprise is coming down."

Though the golfers insist no exertion is required, the hangars smell like workout rooms. An early problem of mats bunching up was remedied when MIU engineers reversed the flow of morning air traffic in the evening sessions.

Team meetings are held in Hipp's "lodge": a converted garage in back of his house. Practicing their swings with phantom clubs, the Pioneers seem to be drifting through a series of ghost moves, blissed out in self-forgetfulness.

Hipp's most harmonious lodge meeting convened before the 1996 state finals. "We spent two hours here, clarifying our intentions," he says. Hipp recorded those intentions on a large white pad:

"I want to finish in the top five."

"I want to place first."

"I want to shoot a 69."

After an hour and a half of clarification, Duveyoung said, "This isn't working for me. I don't see anything up there that will make me play my best." Hipp tore the sheet off the pad and let it feather to the floor. Half an hour later, the golfers had hammered out their true intent: "Our commitment is to give the sincerest expressions of our hearts."

The Pioneers played the championship tournament expressively and with heart. "We were one big team," recalls Duveyoung. "Other schools tended to be just a bunch of individuals." He shot a 76, losing a playoff for the state individual title. Schechtman was fourth with a 79. Fifth was teammate Ted Hirsch, who shot a 43 on the front nine, then steadied and came home with a 37 on the back. "Even after that 43, Ted recognized he was still in the game," Hipp says. "His only goal was to express his heart sincerely."

Buoyed by the team's success, MIU built the Royal Lotus Golf Course and Country Club, a semiprivate course in Fairfield. Hipp was named the club pro. "The course should exert a subtle energy," he says. "The energy would cause golfers to be happier, play better, and be more enlightened." Consultants from the Maharishi Sthapatya Veda Institute were enlisted to ensure that the design conformed to ancient Vedic principles of directionality and proportionality and that the course radiated maximum enlightenment. But the consultants, who at first knew nothing about golf, advised that every hole face either north or east. "Unfortunately, if you think about it, you wouldn't ever get back to the clubhouse," Hipp says. "Unless one clubhouse was in Iowa and one in Minnesota."

When this small detail was resolved, Hipp was free to dream about opening day: "I imagined Maharishi standing on the first tee in his *dhoti*, hitting the first drive." Though Maharishi didn't show up, Hipp says, the late Netherlands-based ascetic was a fan of the game. "Ah, golf!" Maharishi once mused. "A very royal sport. Just walking along the green fairways." And as we all know, it's the walking—the space between—where the real game is played.

ONLY THE LONELY

LAS VEGAS, NEVADA

The slot machines that flank the gaming tables at the MGM Grand Hotel & Casino in Las Vegas are an army of greedy, slightly insolent robots, coughing up winners with a consumptive clunk. In the wee small hours of the morning, when the action on the slots has begun to slow down, a stranger in the night arrives to heat things up. He ambles by the Directors Club, past the Studio Cafe, and through the gaggle of saints and sinners, acknowledging them with a curt nod.

The stranger wears an exquisitely cut Italian suit, a hat set at a jaunty angle, and the thin, weary, seen-it-all expression common to homicide detectives, White House correspondents, and the chairman of the board. Easing up to a blackjack table, he slides a small Everest of chips across the green baize and narrows his baby blues. The dealer snaps two cards toward him—one up, one down. One up is the ace of hearts; one down, the king of spades. "Ring-a-ding ding," sighs the stranger. "Ring-a-ding ding."

Faux Blue Eyes set the tone for the inaugural Frank Sinatra Las Vegas Celebrity Classic, a faux golf tournament played by faux notables in the faux entertainment—or is it faux-entertainment?—capital of the world. Conceived some two years before Sinatra's trip to the Big Casino in the Sky, the celeb-am featured some of the smallest names in the industry: Tom Dreesen, Norm Crosby, Jack Carter, Mike Connors, Hal Linden, Mac Davis, David Cassidy, Robert Stack, Kathleen Sullivan, Vic Damone, Susan Anton, Jerry Vale, Robert Goulet, and other luminaries too faded to mention. Though pictured in the event's "celebrity portfolio," *Laugh-In*'s Arte Johnson had to beg out at the last minute. "An Arte Johnson is hard to replace," said one duffer. Evidently, Ruth Buzzi was unavailable.

For a guy who hated to play golf, Sinatra had almost as many eponymous tournaments as wives. The Frank Sinatra Open Invitational kicked off in 1964 in Palm Springs. But the event fizzed out a year earlier than his 24-month marriage to Mia Farrow—officials concluded the desert needed only one tour stop and picked the more savory Bob Hope to host it. Since 1992, the town has harbored the Frank Sinatra Desert Classic, a small affair remembered mostly for the fact that Ol' Blue Eyes gave his final performance there in 1995.

The last major triangulation of Sinatra, golf, and Vegas

was in 1967. Angered at being denied credit at the Sands, Sinatra steered a golf cart into a plate-glass window. A brawl ensued with the casino's manager, who slugged The Voice in the chops, knocking the caps off his two front teeth. Of course, the Vegas of Sinatra's Rat Pack—a Vegas that Hunter S. Thompson described with much fear and loathing as an Inferno of Hell—is long gone. The Pack's Xanadu, the Sands Hotel, was demolished in 1996 to make room for a theme-parked megaresort. Sin City is now the City of Entertainment, and the skin trade has been supplanted by skins games.

MAY 26, 4 P.M. THE MGM GRAND.

Wayne Newton's skin is a shade of red that doesn't appear on any color chart. His cheeks look as if they've been exposed to the same radioactive isotope that spawned Godzilla. The Midnight Idol stands at the entrance of the Studio A ballroom in all his nuclear glory for a ribbon-cutting ceremony at the Sinatra memorabilia exhibit. "I never asked to cohost this tournament," he says ominously. "The Sinatras *told* me to."

Spread out in 10 glass display cases, the mementos offer a splintered and kaleidoscopic but wide-angled view of Sinatra's life. Despite the mausoleum lighting and the funereal potted palms, the grand array is dazzling: photographs, albums, magazine covers, 78s, 33s, 45s, medallions, busts, buttons, paperbacks, comic books, film posters (including one in French for that Rat Pack classic *Les 7 Voleurs de Chicago*), and the program from his September 8,

1935 breakout performance—as a member of the Hoboken Four—with Major Bowes.

There's enough sheet music—"The Coffee Song," "The Huckle-Buck," "Don't Cry Joe (Let Her Go, Let Her Go, Let Her Go)"—to supply a small orchestra. But not a single toupee, and no golf clubs, trophies, or scorecards.

"I do have a golf ball with 'Francis Albert Sinatra' engraved on it," offers archivist Ric Ross. "The fact is, Sinatra wasn't much of a golfer. He tried it on and off for 35 years. He never perfected his game, and anything he didn't do well, he didn't do. So he gave it up for good in the early '80s."

True, Sinatra was the world's foremost swinger. But *Swing Easy*, *A Swingin' Affair* and *Songs for Swingin' Lovers!* were not instructional LPs. And swingin' brass is not quite the same thing as swingin' titanium.

MAY 27, NOON. THE LIBERACE MUSEUM.

Eyeing a black, floor-length mink cape studded with 100,000 Austrian rhinestones, executive director Myron Martin claims Liberace never wanted his own celebrity golf tournament. "If Lee had hosted one, it would have been as much about showmanship as sportsmanship," says Martin. "Carts would need extra batteries to power the candelabras mounted on their roofs."

Martin doubts Liberace had any great passion for the sport. "I do know he was a guy who tried everything," he says, barely containing a grin. "If Lee owned clubs, he probably adorned them with bugle beads and painted them in brilliant colors."

But how would Liberace have played in a 200-pound cape? A delicious smile creases Martin's face. "Very well," he says.

MAY 28, 8 P.M. POOLSIDE. DESERT INN.

Back in the Stone Age of Celebrity, a star was anyone famous enough to have his 8x10 nailed to the wall of the Stage Deli in New York. Today it's anyone whose renown can be summed up in three words. Sinatra was one of the few three-worders who actually evolved: from bow-tie boy to wounded torch singer to scotch-fueled swinger to dissipated saloon singer ... Most of the famous who show up at the pairings party are of the 15-minute variety.

"I performed on *The Tonight Show* 59 times," says Tom Dreesen maybe 59 times. "I was Sinatra's opening act for 13 years. In fact, I was a pallbearer at his funeral." And what do golf celebs have than noncelebs don't? "A celebrity," muses Dreesen, "is someone who has been celebrated."

Dreesen competes in 12 events a year on the Celebrity Players Tour, an athlete-heavy alliance that requires a handicap of 10 or less—which is about 30 fewer strokes than the handicaps of much of the Sinatra tournament's field. "I'm the CPT's leading money winner among stand-up comics," Dreesen says, without a hint of irony. He's also the CPT's only stand-up comic, not counting the unintentionally hilarious Dan Quayle.

"What's my handicap?" Dreesen repeats. "Being half-Irish and half-Italian. There's a constant war going on inside me."

He says this while leaning against a buffet table festively trimmed with potatoes: Idahos, russets, and Mr. Potato Heads—some wearing little plastic spectacles, others carrying little plastic handbags. On the far end of this spud-o-rama is Crosby, the celebrated funnyman of *Merv Griffin Show* fame.

So what's your handicap, Norm?

"My hearing. I can't hear."

Norm Crosby says Sinatra never cared about golf. "He'd miss a shot and laugh," says the Master of Malapropisms. "If he was too tired or too hot or felt like getting a drink, he'd say, 'Let's quit.' Didn't matter if he was having the best game of his life. And that was pretty much his philosophy of life."

On the other hand, Jack Carter, the celebrated funnyman of *Viva Las Vegas* fame, doesn't believe Sinatra ever played golf. "Frank was never even on a course," he insists. "The only ball he ever hit was into a bottle."

By the way, Jack, what's your handicap?

"I'm Jewish, and I've got hemorrhoids."

MAY 29, 11 A.M. STALLION MOUNTAIN COUNTRY CLUB. Noncelebs pay $3,500 for the privilege of schmoozing celebs in the two-day Classic. The proceeds mostly benefit the Barbara Sinatra Children's Center in Rancho Mirage, California. "The rest goes to the mentally challenged," says Dreesen. "They're the ones who provided all the volunteers for this tournament."

A pro shop employee who identifies himself only as

"Harry" is one of four noncelebs teamed in a best-ball scramble with Carter. "I used to run a brothel," allows Harry, the uncelebrated funnyman. "But I've clean up my act, and now I'm a male prostitute."

Carter lines up a 10-foot putt and taps his ball toward the hole. It starts right and shimmies left, missing the cup by two feet. "I sliced it," he quips. "Anyone here ever slice his putts?"

Nobody laughs.

Carter reaches into his pocket, takes out another ball and drops it onto the green. "This is what you do when you slice a putt," he cackles, slapping the ball holeward. It slices roughward. "Now that's what I call slicing a putt!"

Nobody laughs.

Has Carter been a load of laughs? "Not yet," says Harry, "but we're still holding out hope."

MAY 29, 2 P.M. STALLION MOUNTAIN COUNTRY CLUB.

Though the Classic is free to the public, the fairways are anything but mobbed. At this event, the volunteer and the two autograph hounds at the 14th green on the west course constitute a gallery. One hound— a middle-aged woman— thrusts a yellowing publicity still at Cassidy. "I was so in love with you when I was eight," she tells the celebrated singer of *Partridge Family* fame.

As a three-cart procession approaches the tee box, the mentally-challenged volunteer yells: "He's a *bad* mutha."

"Shut your mouth," snaps the celeb in lead cart. He's none other than Richard Roundtree, the celebrated action hero of *Shaft* fame.

"I go along with this theme-song stuff," he says. "As long as the fans aren't laughing *at* me."

MAY 30, 1 P.M. STALLION MOUNTAIN COUNTRY CLUB.

A table near the 18th tee on the west course is strewn with pamphlets for the Limited Edition Sinatra humidor, a "magnificent work of art" that retails for $1,995 and comes with a precision hygrometer, brass hydrant hinges, and the Sinatra family crest. For another $1,000 they'll throw in 100 "signature" cigars, though under the circumstances, Sinatra's autograph may be hard to authenticate.

A booth near the 18th tee on the north course features an Elvis impersonator, a different Elvis from the one who stalked celebrated supermodel Carol Alt on the west course. "We took care of the Bad Elvis," says a security guard. "Got in his face, and he left the building." So to speak.

The showgirls who have been posing with golfers at 13 west have their own hazard to contend with: Robert Goulet.

"He kept pinching our butts," says Showgirl #1.

"I mean, what were we supposed to do," says Showgirl #2, "slap Robert Goulet?"

MAY 30, 2 P.M. STALLION MOUNTAIN COUNTRY CLUB.

Pppppttttt ...

Whenever one of the noncelebs in Leslie Nielsen's fivesome tees off or putts or chips out of the sand, the sound of protracted flatulence issues from his hip pocket. "I've got a bad case of gas," deadpans the celebrated funny man of *Mr. Magoo* fame. "Must have been the barbecue sauce I had in the tent on the last hole."

Ppppptttt ...

"Golf teaches you patience and insensitivity."

Ppppptttt ...

"You have to learn to be insensitive."

Ppppptttt ...

"It's an art."

Ppppptttt ...

MAY 30, 7 P.M. MGM GRAND.

It's not without a certain irony that the Sinatra tribute culminates in a black-tie gala at the MGM Grand. Sinatra was fired by MGM in 1950 after making a crack about the mistress of studio head Louis B. Mayer. The only remaining link between the MGM Grand and Sinatra is the Studio Cafe's movie-themed menu. You can order an $18.95 Anchors Aweigh (surf-and-turf kabob) with a $7.95 High Society (turkey-breast club sandwich) on the side. Dessert options include the On the Town cheesecake ($3.75). Add another buck if you want the cherry fruit topping.

Alas, for those who feel like Chinese, the cafe offers no Manchurian Candidate. And the indigestion lasts from here to eternity.

THE FEHERTY WAY

ULSTER, IRELAND

rish character, says Ulsterman David Feherty, is like Irish weather: rich in variety, but lacking stamina—it sticks to nothing for long. When Feherty, golf's greatest Irish character, was a wee lad of nine, he had just enough stamina to caddy for his old man at the Bangor Golf Club in County Down. William Feherty's foursome included his physician, whose advice for the elder Feherty's insomnia had been, "Play a round in your head." While walking the fairway at the 4th hole, the doctor asked William, "Did you sleep any better?"

"Not really," said William. "I played great until the 3rd tee shot, which I sliced into the trees. I was awake all night looking for the ball."

More than four decades later, David Feherty gleefully

calls this the defining moment of his life. "I realized that everything my dad and his friends said was total bull," he says, "and that there were more important things than sport. That one quip spurred me on to be a wiseass."

What Feherty defines as wiseass others call a singular genius for making fun of everything pompous, humorless, and boring. In short, the PGA Tour. Over the last decade this onetime European Tour player has become the most entertaining TV analyst this side (or maybe the far side) of Bob Newhart. Whereas the humor of his CBS teammate Gary McCord can sound slavishly contrived, Feherty comes off as unaffected and unrehearsed. "David's an amoeba," says retired CBS golf producer Frank Chirkinian. "There's form, yet no form. He's so spontaneous that you never know what's coming next."

A few Fehertyisms that have come and gone:

"The only time Nick Faldo opens his mouth is to change feet."

"On a bad day my swing was like a privy door on a trawler in the middle of the Atlantic."

"So many born-again players have credited the Lord after victories that Jack Nicklaus' record for major titles is in jeopardy. God is already halfway there."

Feherty is shamelessly willing to go in for absolute nonsense—not only to be utterly silly but also to display outrageously bad taste. Who else can get away with saying a certain pro "couldn't hit a tile floor with a bladder full of beer" or likening a ball smacked off a club face to "hot snot out of a chrome nostril"?

His pinball-machine mind lacks an off switch. "David is the kind of commentator—and it's very, very rare—whom people will tune in to just to watch," says Rick Gentile, the former executive producer of CBS Sports, who hired Feherty in 1996. "Viewers know that even if a tournament isn't compelling, David will be."

Feherty *compels* his way into the nation's living rooms. CBS bills him as an on-course reporter, though he prefers the lesser designation of "mobile microphone holder." He'll relay how far a shot has been hit, describe the lie, and identify what club a golfer is using. "I'm just a fairway creeper trying to stay out of the way," he says in a voice that doesn't so much speak as croon. "A chimp could do my job. The network can't find one with a foreign accent."

Off camera Feherty's wit is even more mordant. Among his dislikes: sweet wines, being away from home, accommodations at the British Open ("I always get stuck in rooms with nylon sheets and shiny toilet paper," he says), food that looks up at him from the table, unplayable lies, the film *Striptease*, the actress Sandra Bullock, the actor Tom Arnold, and the singer Mariah Carey ("She sings like a mouse on acid," he says).

Among his likes: Beamish stout, being home, Donegal sunsets, jalapeño peppers, 10-inch eagle putts, the book *Striptease*, the actress Catherine Zeta-Jones, the actor Liam Neeson, and the singer Bob Dylan ("Golf is like a Dylan song," he muses. "You don't have to understand it to enjoy it").

Golf is something he neither likes nor dislikes. "It falls in the middle," he says. "I've never had an overwhelming passion for the game. One of my greatest problems as a player was that I couldn't be that serious. I was more interested in behaving badly. All that work and practice is overrated. It occupies a lot of time that could be spent drinking beer or telling jokes or laughing good-naturedly at other people's failures."

Generally, the failures Feherty laughs at are his own. He's exceedingly gracious and excellent company, a tireless raconteur. "Let me tell you a story," is perhaps his trademark phrase. He'll yammer on forever about his old sports car, a 1990 AC Cobra, a "roller skate with 350 horsepower that spat out unburned fuel on the downshift, was so percussive that when you turned on the ignition, it would trigger every car alarm within five miles, and got four miles to the gallon—on the highway. It's the only car I've ever driven in which you could watch the fuel gauge moving." Then there's his former caddy, Rodney, who used to "stay up all night drinking cleaning products," and the Porsche that Feherty totaled at the 1992 Irish Open when "a wall leapt out in front of me" and the Senior tour player who "has a recurring nightmare of getting in a plane crash and having his body found in coach."

In the harbor town of Bangor, near Belfast, sarcasm was a staple of the Feherty household. David still remembers the night Da crawled home from a pub and told Ma, "Sorry I'm late, dear. Is my dinner warm?"

"Yes," she said evenly. "It's in the dog."

David was William and Violet's only son, the middle child of three. A choirboy at six, he was trained to be an opera singer. "When I reached puberty, my voice broke," he says. "From then on I sounded like a baritone held very tightly by the scrotum." Today he sings just to punish his kids. "It's so much more effective than spanking."

A Protestant, he mingled with Catholics only when on the links. "We'd shoot par in the morning and each other at night," he says. In 1976, with his handicap down to five, the 17-year-old Feherty quit school and turned pro. As he tells it, the idea came one day while sitting in geography class. "I figured I'd learn more about a certain country if I visited it," he says, "so I went to see the headmaster, and within a few days I was an assistant pro in England."

During his 20 years as a Tour pro Feherty was decent if unspectacular, winning five events in Europe and 10 worldwide.

His first two victories came in 1986 at the Italian and Scottish Opens. "It felt pretty weird," he says. "I didn't think I was that good." He wasn't. Yet in 1991 he made the Ryder Cup team that narrowly lost the War by the Shore at Kiawah Island, South Carolina, and beat Payne Stewart in the singles. "On my first putt everything moved except my bowels," he says. "It took about four years to stop shaking."

A few years later, at 36, he moved with his wife and two sons from Bangor to Dallas. Or, rather, he followed his wife and two sons to Dallas. She had been unhappy in Northern Ireland, and he would be equally unhappy in the U.S. He supported his family by playing on the PGA Tour. In his first year, 1994, he earned $178,501 and placed 100th on the money list. Then his marriage and game fell apart simultaneously. His wife left and took the boys with her. "I was devastated, depressed, and broke," he says. "I spent entire days in bed. The last place I wanted to be was on a golf course."

His appetite for the game gone, Feherty went on what he called the divorce diet—coffee, cigarettes, Advil, and alcohol. "If it was under the sink," he says, "I'd drink it." He tried to run away from his problems, literally, jogging more than 100 miles a week. "I lost 40 pounds," he says. "A hundred and fifty if you include my wife."

Feherty's dark night of the soul lasted a year, until he met an interior decorator named Anita Schneider. "It was a blind date," he says. "I was blind drunk." The evening lasted all of half an hour. A few days later Feherty phoned her, pleading for a second chance. He got one, at a Texas Rangers game. "I showed up sober," he says, "and made a better impression." He gave up smoking, stopped running, and remarried in the spring of 1996. The couple's first child, Erin, was born two years later.

Feherty entered the public consciousness at the 1990 World Cup in Orlando, where he shot a 63 and famously compared the Grand Cypress course to one of those hot-air hand dryers found in public rest rooms: "It's a great idea and everybody uses it once, but never again. It takes too long." The next year, during the PGA at Crooked Stick, he cracked to a TV interviewer, "This course is so long that figuring distances on some holes, you have to reckon in the curvature of the earth."

During the 1995 Sprint International, at the height of Feherty's troubles, McCord invited him up to the CBS booth. Feherty was still playing competitively, but not competing much. (He finished the year 166th on the money list, then missed the four-round cut at Q school a few months later and lost his Tour card.) McCord asked Feherty if he would consider someday joining the CBS team, and the next spring, at the 1996 Doral-Ryder Open in Miami, Feherty auditioned with the network. Later that season, at the PGA in Louisville, he bummed a ride to dinner with CBS executive producer Lance Barrow. "Tell me," he asked Barrow, "how much money can I make doing TV full time?"

Barrow told him. "Hmm ... sounds okay," said Feherty. "When can I start?"

By late December, Feherty had quit playing and had signed a three-year deal with CBS worth more than $800,000. He made his first big splash the following February at Pebble Beach, snagging Tiger Woods after Woods had gambled in the final round and reached the 18th green with a three-wood. Feherty asked, "Were you concerned at all by that big blue thing to the left?" He meant the Pacific Ocean.

Feherty still makes waves. At the 1997 John Deere Classic in Coal Valley, Illinois, he commentated from a tower overlooking the 16th green. In heat that would be considered mild only on Mercury, Feherty kept cool in a maroon polo shirt, khaki shorts, white socks, and Birkenstocks. "There's Fuzzy Zoeller," he told TV-land. "You'd have to assume he's both warm and Fuzzy. He may just be sticky and Fuzzy, although that's probably an oxymoron."

The camera panned to an enormous tractor near the 11th hole. A fellow analyst asked, "David, have you ever been on a tractor?"

"No," he replied, "but I've been on a backhoe."

"Where?"

At that moment, a mike at the 16th recorded the loud, unmistakable sound of what Feherty would later describe as a "Fuzzy trouser burp."

Feherty remained uncharacteristically silent.

"After Fuzzy farted, my train of thought was backhoe, back passage, backside," he explained. "I was thinking I probably didn't want to take it any farther. As a broadcasting sage once told me, 'They'll never criticize you for saying too little.' "

COME FLY WITH ME

OXFORD, ENGLAND

Death by bacon.

That was the sentence Redmond O'Hanlon meted out for the botfly digging through my left wrist. The little larva had begun to freeload off me while I was walking the Summit golf course on the east bank of the Panama Canal and now, three weeks later, was making like Charles Bronson, the Tunnel King, in *The Great Escape*. "The path it has traced through your skin," noted O'Hanlon, "is not unlike the layout of the Road Hole at St. Andrews."

O'Hanlon, the peerless British travel writer and naturalist, is something of a connoisseur of the tropical botfly. Though he has never had one burrow into him, he has seen plenty while tramping through the world's most remote jungles. "This is the first live botfly that's ever visited my home," he says excitedly in his Oxfordshire study. "I'm truly delighted!"

Exactly what the author of *No Mercy* finds delightful about botflies eludes me. If you think horseflies have bad manners, you should see botflies. An adult looks something like a bumblebee, if a bumblebee were covered in unbristled black hair and had bright green headlamps for eyes. The horse botfly—known to Socratic scholars as the gadfly—leaves about 500 eggs on its victim's forelegs, nose, and lips. The larvae remain in the eggs until the horse licks itself, whereby—stimulated by moisture and friction—they emerge, get swallowed, and spend the next 11 months dizzily cruising the horse's alimentary canal. Cattle botflies bore into the hide of a cow, then bum around subcutaneously for a few months before settling in Clarabelle's back. The hideous lump each larva causes is called a warble. The deer nose botfly is supposed to be the fastest of the flying insects, with a top speed of about 50 miles an hour. They're swifter, but not nastier, than the sheep botfly, which leaves nits in the nostrils of its host, causing a nervous condition called blind staggers. The less said about the rodent botfly the better. (All right, if you really have to know, it attacks the testicles of squirrels and emasculates them.)

Which brings us, inevitably, to the human botfly—a circumspect little critter that attacks tropical duffers. The female attaches her eggs to mosquitoes and stable flies, which do the dirty work for her. Ninety-eight point six turns out to be the perfect temperature to hatch botfly eggs, and the larvae enter your skin. After 40 days of squiggling, the botfly grub emerges. The grub becomes a pupa and then a fly and then ... well ... here we go again. *Zzz zzz zzz zzz zzt*, says the female botfly. The more ill-humored females say simply *zzt*. Females tend to be sly and conniving; males, downright irresponsible. Many male bugs procreate and die. The male botfly procreates and procreates. No wonder we hear so much these days about the breakdown of botfly family values!

I feel a certain affection for the orphaned Panamanian bot fly that has taken up residence in my arm. Ennis, I call him, after the Montana golf club at which I hit my first wormburner. As he writhes in my wrist, Ennis makes tortured little semaphores. A week before I arrived at Redmond's, he had formed an "S." Yesterday, a "P." Today, Ennis has outdone himself: taken the rather complicated shape of a "Q." I remind O'Hanlon of how Lassie once alerted her dim human masters to a blaze in the barn by spelling out "F-I-R-E" in Timmy's oatmeal. "If memory serves, Lassie practiced orthography in pinhead oats," O'Hanlon corrects me, adding: "P-I-N-H-E-A-D."

O'Hanlon is a large, exuberant, and enormously funny man, curious and observant, with thickets of gray hair, a reckless optimism, and an undepletable fund of anecdotes. The most prickly involves the candiru, a toothpick-shaped one-inch-long catfish native to the Amazon. The candiru can follow the scent of urine up a victim's urethra, where it anchors itself by flaring its spiny fins. "Nothing can be done," says O'Hanlon, who rigged up an anti-candiru condom by sewing a tea strainer into the cup of a jockstrap. "The pain, apparently, is spectacular. You must get to a hospital before your bladder bursts." The only certain method of candiru removal is penile amputation (again, if you must know).

While mulling how best to extract the *Dermatobia hominis* from my wrist, O'Hanlon suddenly barges off to another room. He returns with a travel book about South America titled *Jaguar*. "When I was natural history editor of the *London Times Literary Supplement*, I devoted an entire page to *Jaguar*," says O'Hanlon. "In one chapter, a botfly bites the author's girlfriend on the nipple, and the author is called on to squeeze the bot fly out. It was all extremely erotic."

Endless debugging stories are one of the burdens a botfly-bearer must suffer. A few days earlier, a friend had related the tale of a Los Angeleno who had been de-botted by a pet parrot. Another friend told me about a Manhattanite whose Costa Rican botfly had festered into a great blue welt. One day, as the New Yorker attended a ball game at Yankee Stadium, the grub emerged and buzzed off. Whether the infield fly rule was invoked is unclear.

Within O'Hanlon's cottage, a pleasant disorder reigns. Books and magazines overwhelm the first floor, filling up shelves, the ground, and even the stairs. Everything that could possibly hold a book is pressed into service. Odd and exotic treasures line the walls (his raffine taste in golf clubs extends to hickory-shafted spoons, cleeks, and baffies). On a mantel near a stuffed pelican is a Maxwell House can containing the charred foot of his best friend at Oxford, who burned himself to death at 24. On another, a carved wooden totem, draped in a sinister ribbon. "It's a kind of Congolese voodoo doll," O'Hanlon says. "Each knot in the ribbon signifies a successful death." (There are 12 knots.) Reposing atop his desk is the skull of a howler monkey. Local Amazonian custom dictated that he suck out the monkey's eyes. When he complied, a local groaned, "How revolting! You white men will do anything to be loved."

Surely, O'Hanlon will. Unbuttoning his shirt, he pulls forth another magic talisman—a lump of string and monkey fur wrapped around a child's finger. He has carried the pouch around for the last seven years. "I realize this fetish is on very marshy ground intellectually," he says. "But it doesn't matter if you believe it or not—it plays straight into the subconscious." When he briefly lost the totem in a restaurant at the Rotterdam Golfclub Kralingen, he broke into a cold sweat.

O'Hanlon has roosted in this quiet corner of the Southeast of England for two decades. Every so often he grabs some bug spray and a sheaf of photocopied ornithological classics and flutters off into the wild. In 1983, it was the Borneo rain forest. Three years later, the Amazon basin. More recently, the swampland of the Congo—a quagmire, he says, not unlike the second cut of rough at Carnoustie. Upon his return, the Cambridge University biology professor plays every local golf course from Southfield to Hinksey Heights before chronicling his adventures in books that twin scholarship with ensemble comedy and leave readers convinced they would rather gulp down a monkey's eyeball than follow him one step of the way. O'Hanlon's appreciation of suffering borders on the masochistic. "It's part of a particular brand of Anglicanism," he explains. "Unless you're suffering, it can't be real."

O'Hanlon believes a botfly is a gift that must be shared with his loved one. "Belinda!" he shouts to his wife. "Come look at this."

"Look at what?" shouts Belinda from the kitchen.

"Ennis." Belinda comes and looks. Redmond says, "A handsome botfly, is he not?"

"Ughhh," said Belinda.

Redmond furrows his eyebrows into a long smudge, and forms a tent with his fingertips. "Belinda," he asks, "do we have any fat?"

"Fat?"

"Yes."

"No."

"What about bacon, then?"

"Sorry. We're all out of that as well."

"Are you sure? I bought a rasher this morning. It should be in the fridge."

Belinda sprints to the refrigerator, finds the rasher, and unwraps it. "A botfly pierces your skin and breathes through its anus," explains Redmond, grabbing the slab of bacon, peeling off a slice, and draping it over my wrist. "This bacon ought to smother Ennis," he says. Then he wraps gauze around the bacon and adhesive tape around the gauze. I ask, "How long should I keep my arm baconed?"

"Yes, how long should you bacon it?" O'Hanlon says distractedly, spooning out a word at a time. "Hmmm ... I guess until you can stand the stench no longer."

Which turns out to be a day and a half. When I depork myself, Ennis is gone. And my wrist has a nice hickory scent. But two days later, another tunnel appears, this one not unlike the 17th hole of the Players Championship at Sawgrass. Is Ennis back? Or is this his brother, Dennis? I re-bacon. For three days this time. Again, no sign of Ennis. Or, for that matter, Dennis.

A day passes. A week. Two weeks. Surely, I think, I'm finally rid of my botfly. But I'm wrong. Sixteen days after the disappearance of Ennis (or Dennis), Glynnis shows up trailing Hole No. 1 at Royal Melbourne. That's it! Whatever's gotten under my skin has got to go. I jab a needle into Ennis/Dennis/Glynnis. Twenty times, maybe 30. Then I pry out the carcass and soak my throbbing wrist in hydrogen peroxide.

Ennis, anyone?

STEALTH BOMBER

O f all the Cinderella stories in sports, the one that unfolded at the 2006 HSBC Women's World Match Play Championship may have been the first to involve a genuine Cinderella. Brittany Lincicome, virtually a scullery maid among the glamorous young princesses of the LPGA, won her first tournament by beating six players head-to-head, including three of the Tour's top eight.

An ebullient 19-year-old known the length and breadth of Seminole, Florida, Lincicome ran the table on several generations at Hamilton Farm. Her victims ranged in age from 16 (Michelle Wie) to 46 (Juli Inkster, who had won four LPGA tournaments before Lincicome was born). "Tomorrow I'll wake up and say, 'Did I just dream that?'" she said on Sunday after drubbing Inkster 3 and 2 in the final. If the glass slipper fits, Brittany, wear it.

With her blonde ponytail streaming like a horse's mane, Lincicome is as fanciful as a character in a storybook, and as whimsical: Her socks have itty-bitty Winnie the Pooh pom-poms stitched on the heels. "The pom-poms keep the footsies from disappearing into my FootJoys," she more or less explained.

Lincicome took up golf at 9 and made a name for herself—albeit a small one—on the junior circuit. Her parents ran a day-care center in Pinellas Park and couldn't afford to send her to an academy or hire a coach. Lincicome's father, Tom, became her caddy. "It was always Dad and I doing it—the homeschool thing and all the sacrifices," she says. Lincicome turned pro in 2005 and helped bankroll her rookie season by babysitting. On the Tour, in the shadow of teen prodigies Wie, Paula Creamer, and Morgan Pressel, she earned $127,452 but little recognition.

Lincicome qualified for the Match Play on the strength of a seventh-place finish at the 2006 U.S. Women's Open in Newport, Rhode Island. She carried a share of the lead into the final round but double-bogeyed the 7th hole, then bogeyed the 8th and ballooned to a 78.

Her stumble at the Open made Lincicome, seeded 39th, something of a dark horse, as the first three rounds pretty much shaped up as the Women's World Mismatch Play Championship. The top five seeds breezed into the quarterfinals: Only one match went the full 18 holes. Annika Sorenstam's third-round laugher with Brittany Lang ended on 13.

But the wide fairways and long par-5's of Hamilton Farm favored the long-ball game of Lincicome, who ranked No. 2 on tour in driving distance at 281.7 yards. "If it didn't snow in New Jersey during the winter," she said, "I would probably move here."

That was the second year the event was held at the hilly course, and the last. Club members objected to everything from the LPGA's hefty site fee to the public's trampling the club's well-manicured bentgrass. Of the 6,700 tramplers on hand for the Saturday matches, roughly 6,672 were there to shadow Wie. Among them was Nike founder Phil Knight, who had signed Wie to a reported $5 million endorsement deal.

Fresh off her tie for third at the U.S. Women's Open, the field's youngest player arrived eager to match wits with her elders. She spotted Candy Hannemann 10 years, but the brittle Brazilian got bounced 5 and 3.

Next was Christina Kim, a chatty Californian who considers Wie a close friend. Regardless, Wie gave Kim—as she did all her opponents—the silent treatment and let her driver do the talking, bombing it 30 yards ahead of Kim on most fairways and storming to a 3 and 2 win. She then played long ball to top former No. 1 Se Ri Pak 2 and 1, and run her overall record on the par-5's to 9-1-2.

In the quarters Wie finally met her Match Play match. Staying with Wie bomb for bomb, the 5'10" Lincicome blew away her foe with three birdies on the first five holes to build an advantage she would never surrender. Lincicome had a harder time with Lorena Ochoa, the Tour's leading money winner. Lincicome twice went 2 up on her Bible-study partner and twice lost back-to-back holes. When both players parred the 18th, they moved to the 10th, where Lincicome sank a 20-footer for birdie and Ochoa sank her head after missing from 19 feet.

Then Lincicome was off to the final against Inkster. A nonpareil match player with a 5-1 record in Solheim Cup singles, Inkster had upended Sorenstam on the 18th hole of the quarters before crushing Creamer 5 and 4 in the semis.

In the final, though, Inkster fell behind when Lincicome reached the green of the 533-yard, par-5 2nd hole in two and two-putted for a birdie. Aided by her father, an expert reader of curlicue putts, Lincicome won holes 3 and 4 with pars and had a 5-up lead after eight. When Inkster conceded a par putt on the 16th, it was all over.

"Coming through all those players and beating all of them, it means I actually did deserve to win this tournament," Lincicome said. Her $500,000 take was $107,742 more than she had earned in all 33 of her previous Tour starts and $499,950 more than she got for her best night babysitting.

THE OTHER BOMBERS

BRONX, NEW YORK

hristopher Columbus High has the air of a besieged bunker. Security guards man every entrance and exit of this public school, like sentries on perimeter defense. Cops troop back and forth in the halls, ready to swat the cap off any student impertinent enough to wear one. To get inside the lines, be prepared to give your name, rank, and serial number.

On a dare, 15-year-old sophomore Johnathan Rodriguez tried to slip through the metal detector in the lobby with his golf bag. The clubs triggered an alarm louder than any Bronx cheer. "If 14 metal poles hadn't set that thing off, it would've been funny," Johnathan says.

Johnathan and his buddies on the Columbus golf team have been setting off bells and whistles since the turn of the new century. In 1999, the team's first season since the sport was axed in 1987, Columbus was 5-1 in intraborough match play and shared the Bronx schoolboy title. In 2000, the scruffy squad of mostly first- and second-generation immigrants had that honor all to itself, running its string of regular-season victories over Bronx opponents to 11. "At the start of 2000, half our guys didn't know which end of the club to hit the ball with," says Harvey Zarensky, the school's athletic director, "and none had ever set foot on a fairway."

Bosnian refugee Malik Tekesinovic barely knew what the game was. "Where I come from, golf courses don't look like golf courses anymore," says Malik, who grew up on the mean streets of Sarajevo. "The fairways are full of craters from mortar shells, so everybody just plays soccer."

On the mean streets of the Bronx, the sports are baseball, basketball, and football. "That's the extent of it," says Columbus coach Norm Harris. "It's hard to get kids even to think about golf."

Still, eight public high schools in the Bronx offer the sport, which has an even longer tradition in the borough than the Yankees. Babe Ruth used to spend off-days from the House that He Built playing Van Cortlandt Golf Course, the oldest muni in the country. Gene Sarazen learned the game there, and that's where young Chi Chi Rodriguez sandpapered his.

For decades at Columbus, Al Oglio, a health teacher and a dean at the school, coached the sport, which had played a dark role in his family history but which he loved all the same. "Golf killed his twin brother," says gym teacher Bob Gregory. "A ball hit him in the head." Al Oglio died 13 years ago, taking Columbus golf with him.

It wasn't revived until 1999, when Harris walked into the principal's office and offered his services. A retired TWA vice president with a 20 handicap, Harris lives six blocks from the school. Though he had never taught golf, he had plenty of expertise with teenagers. "I've raised seven," he says. "Being able to anticipate and understand teens is a big plus."

Harris is measured, contemplative, and autocratically benign. He rarely raises his voice, whether he's dispensing advice, reprimanding his players or razzing them into fits of helpless laughter. "You've got to be extremely fair and equal to all," says Harris, "no matter how well or badly they play." He calls his team the Bad News Bears.

Besides the obvious derivation, the Bears got their name from Barry (Bear) Raju, the only senior on the '99 team. Raju became a semimythic figure for something he did while mulling the foot-long putt that would propel Columbus into the Public Schools Athletic League playoffs against the top teams from the city's other four boroughs. As he drew back his putter, Raju spied a quarter on the ground. Dropping the club, he crouched and pocketed the coin, not realizing that the quarter was another player's marker.

The current starting five consists of Little Bear (Malik), Care Bear (Vinh Bui), Gummi Bear (Raymond Heard), Tune Bear (Jason Thoman) and Bedtime Bear (Johnathan).

"We call him Bedtime," says Jason, "because he has an 8:30 p.m. curfew."

"Don't broadcast it!" says Johnathan. "Everybody in school will know what time I have to go to sleep."

"So what?" says Jason with an exaggerated shrug. "Now chicks will come up to you and whisper, 'Hey, Bedtime.'"

"It hasn't happened," says Johnathan.

"'Cause before, nobody noticed us," says Jason. "Now we're famous. Now we're the Bronx champs. We are golden gods!"

A mere 18 months before, these golden gods were the greenest on the green. Columbus supplied each player with a set of clubs and a bag to carry them in. They practiced three hours a day, three days a week—twice a week at a driving range and once on a course. Harris had them watch instructional tapes, drive Wiffle balls into nets, chip from varying distances on the school's football field. "They worked their butts off," he says.

The Columbus coach requires not only artistry but sacrifice as well. When Raymond, the team's No. 1 player (he does well to break 100), finished the third quarter with a 63 grade-point average, Harris barred him from the final regular-season match. Hours of extra work raised his grades enough to earn him a spot on the postseason roster. "Ray told me his goal was to make the playoffs," says Harris. "I told him that his goal should be making good marks and then playing golf."

Long-range goals were why Jason joined the team. "People told me you have to play golf if you want to go into business," says the oldest Bear. A big, burly junior among scrawny sophomores, he wears his well-gelled hair swept back in a Rico Suave cut. "They told me most deals are made on the links. Take out your client, let him win, and the deal is done."

Malik signed on because he thought *golf team* would look good on college applications. "Like all the other guys, I live in a roachy apartment," he says. "With all the gunshots, the loud music, the fighting over drugs, it's hard to sleep at night. I thought golf would help get me out of there, so my own kids can live in a better neighborhood."

The gritty public courses on which Columbus has played most of its matches—Van Cortlandt and Pelham—will never be confused with Pebble Beach. Van Cortlandt made headlines in the late '90s when management allowed more than 500 truckloads of construction debris to be dumped at the 17th hole. Pelham had its own unadvertised hazard: Detectives from New York City's auto-crimes division dug up a car buried off the 14th hole.

At Brooklyn's Dyker Beach Golf Course, where the Bears opened the PSAL playoffs last month and where autos are sometimes abandoned in the rough, the club insignia should be a car with a line drawn through it. The Bears take the subway to Dyker—a two-hour ride. "Did you bring your passport?" Harris asks Vinh. The Vietnamese emigre has never been to Brooklyn.

Raymond, the rehabilitated No. 1, misses the train. Nobody even knows if he's been in school that day. Another sophomore, Steven Hernandez, takes his place. As Jason sings to the straphangers with tuneless determination, a woman argues loudly with herself and weeps. Malik gives her a searching look. "What's the matter?" the woman snaps. "Haven't you ever seen an actor rehearse? I'm practicing my lines."

When the Bears reach Dyker, there's no time to warm up. Their opponent, McKee-Staten Island Tech, has been on the putting green for an hour and a half. In contrast to the hip-hop couture of Columbus, the more seasoned Staten Islanders wear color-coordinated outfits. "We come here with our heads held high," intones Johnathan before beginning the nine-hole, team match-play competition. (On each hole, the team with the lowest cumulative score wins.) "If we lose, we walk out with our heads held high."

"Agreed," says Jason. "We can break some kneecaps afterward."

Huffing and heaving, Raymond arrives at Dyker two minutes before the first group tees off. "I got held up in Holocaust class," he alibis. "The teacher wouldn't let me leave." He grabs a club from his ragtag bag and walks, wheezing, to the tee box.

"Asthma," Harris says.

Under tin-gray clouds Raymond addresses the ball, pulls his driver back slowly and then whips it forward on the downswing. *Thump*—his ball weakly slices into an oak about 30 yards away. Staten Island's No. 1—a senior headed for Rutgers—takes a mighty rip that produces a lovely drive right down the middle. "Oh, my god!" says Jason in his low washboard voice.

The tee shot of Malik, the Bears' No. 2, is a popup that wouldn't have made it out of the infield at Yankee Stadium. When the No. 2 Staten Islander chisels 250 yards of real estate off the 363-yard par-4, Jason gasps, "Oh, geez!" After shanking his tee shot onto an adjacent fairway, Jason turns to Harris and extends a hand. "It was a good season," he says.

"It isn't over yet," says the coach. If only that were true. Jason takes seven more strokes, finally rapping in a two-footer for a quadruple bogey. The Bears lose the 1st hole badly. They come a little closer on the 2nd as Malik actually beats his opponent by chipping in a 20-footer from the edge of the green, but alas, the Bears drop the first five holes and lose the match 5 and 4.

Playing out the nine for fun, Vinh—whose robotic stroke seems designed by R2D2—sinks a sensational putt. "The perk of this job is watching one of my guys make a good shot," says Harris, beaming. "It keeps them coming back."

A REAL CROC

CHILILABONBWE, ZAMBIA

The world's toughest eighteen holes lie not along the foggy shores of Pebble Beach or on the wind-whipped undulations of St. Andrews, but rather in the tangled sub-Saharan bush of Chililabombwe, home of the Konkola Golf Club. Chililabombwe, a tiny border town within earshot of the warfare in the Democratic Republic of Congo, is known for its idyllic subtropical climate and for the Konkola Copper Mine, one of the richest on the continent. But the town's golf course—originally called Bancroft Golf Club by its colonial founders and renamed after Zambia won independence in 1964—is clearly the pride of the region.

You really know you're not at Augusta when the scorecard says, "A ball coming to rest in a hippo footprint may be lifted and dropped in the nearest possible position to provide maximum relief." Seven-thousand-pound hippos don't tiptoe; ostriches could nest in the divots they leave. Hippos track across the grounds because the Konkola is near the Kafue River.

Chris Mwaba, the club secretary, sometimes must caution visiting players to watch out for poisonous snakes. Every now and then a duffer bushwhacking through the thigh-high kasensi grass will be confronted by boomslangs, black and green mambas, puff adders, gaboon vipers, or the highly venomous spitting cobra. But perhaps Konkola's greatest challenge is the series of ponds along which ten of its holes are situated. Many a tee shot has gone into the drink, but that's not the biggest problem.

In bold, black letters the scorecard warns "NOTE: BEWARE OF CROCODILES ON HOLES 4, 5, 6, 8, 9, 13, 14, 15, 17 AND 18." To date, almost a half-dozen caddies have been munched while on ball-retrieval expeditions. "Wandering near the water is not the wisest move for a caddy at Konkola," says a club member. "They become easy meat."

Golf is the biggest thing to hit Zambia since Dag Hammerskjold's plane crashed there in 1961. The thirty or so courses that speckle the countryside are among the most exotic in the known world. In Livingstone, golfers risk having their balls swiped by baboons; in Chingola, by vervet monkeys. At the old Kasaba Bay Lodge course, golfers share the fairways with Cape buffalo, hartebeests, wart hogs, hippopotami, elephants, and puku, henna-red antelopes seen mainly in crossword puzzles. Herds of impalas, duikers and black lechwes roam the nine-hole course at the state house in Lusaka. In Ndola, the main obstructions are immense termite mounds. Seventy-two rise from the sandy soil; the 6th hole alone has fourteen. "Zambians call termite towers anthills," says club president John Nkandu. "The hills can grow as high as several stories."

Ndola, Zambia's second-largest city, is where we begin our Konkola chronicle. The town's civic credo, "The Friendly City," is stenciled on an airport wall. Friendly Ndola is. Uneventful it is not. Headlines in one day's newspaper included the following: WIFE EXPOSES BLOOD-SUCKING HUSBAND, SELF-CONFESSED WIZARD GOES IN FOR 2 YEARS and MAGISTRATE SUES OVER COCKROACH IN SOUP.

The counsel offered in the local press can be equally uncommon. Years ago, an editorial in the *Sunday Mail* proposed a novel solution to the Monica Lewinsky scandal: CLINTON SHOULD CONSIDER POLYGAMY.

At Ndola's airport, I consider the Toyotas for rent at Polite Car Hire, politely hire one and cruise the friendly city. In Zambia, traffic lights are called robots, a quaint Britishism that could also describe the cops who mechanically direct traffic. A three-robot town rarely visited by tourists, Ndola is home to the Rhino Lager factory, the Copperbelt Museum, and a colossal Mupapa tree under which Swahili slave traders once sold their captives. The road from Ndola leads through Kitwe ("The Hub of the Copper Belt"), a two-robot hamlet that is home to the Kooky Look! Restaurant, the Lady Blue Hair Salon & Grocery, and the

Three Dice Shell Hole Moth Club, one of the best of its kind. Next stop is Chingola ("The Cleanest Town in Zambia"), home to the Proton Supermarket and some lofty speed bumps.

Mile upon mile of stripped, moon-cratered landscape culminates in Chililabombwe, "The Future of Copper Mining in Zambia." This no-robot hamlet is home to Aunt Millie's Butchery and the Humanism Butchery Mine Market. A red, shadeless road that seems to stretch forever dumps into the gated entrance of the Konkola Golf Club, a neglected outpost of postcolonial decadence. "The fortunes of Zambia's copper industry continue to decline," according to Trish Houston, an unemployed schoolteacher who emigrated from New Zealand in 1978. "It's become harder and harder to keep the club running."

The mine's main shaft was opened in 1957, the same year Konkola was founded. Back then, caddies were black; members, white. "I don't think the club had a no-blacks policy," says Houston, who joined the club in 1980. "It may have had more to do with the fact that the blacks who lived in the area couldn't afford to play. I wouldn't say they were discouraged to play." But she concedes they weren't exactly encouraged to play, either. In fact, no blacks joined the club until several years after independence, in the late 1960s. Only five of the club's current 87 members are white, and only one—Houston—plays regularly.

In the prosperous mid-80s, Konkola hosted a tournament on the PGA's safari circuit. Visiting pros included Nick Faldo, Sandy Lyle, and Ian Woosnam. Houston remembers

Ewen Murray walloping two dozen Titleists into the pond off the 18th tee. "He was trying to hit a croc, and I was pleading, 'Please don't do it!'" she says. "My concern wasn't for the crocs. We just can't get Titleists here."

The club's pro shop has been closed since 1966. To buy a pack of reasonably new Top-Flites, you must drive all the way back to Chingola. Sets of three sell for ten thousand kwacha (roughly five dollars), which also happens to be the monthly dues at Konkola. In case you're planning to visit, the green fee will set you back a hefty 50 cents. At the 19th hole, the bar food of choice—caterpillar grubs—are free. Club member Charles Sihole likes them fried. His golfing buddy Mike Musopelo prefers his boiled. "They absorb salt better," he explains. "Boiled is much better than raw." His caddy, Solomon Pliri, says grubs taste best floating in a glass of beer. (I find beer-soaked grubs only slightly less palatable than soup-soaked cockroaches.)

Beer is said to be the major obsession of Zambians. In his African travelogue *North of South*, Shiva Naipaul wrote that Zambians are purported to be second only to Australians in beer consumption. (He also reports the not unrelated rumor that Zambia boasts the world's highest road-accident rate.) A substantial store of the beverage is stashed in the clubhouse kitchen. Beer burglars broke in every Christmas Eve—until the early 1990s, when a cop shot a thief as he climbed through a window. Did the thief die?

"No," says Musopelo. "But his leg was amputated." Bush-golf justice is brutal and absolute.

The course is as formidable as its ponds are forbidding.

Par is 73, a stroke over the course record. The layout is 7,408 yards. Until recently, the 620-yard 4th hole was said to be the longest in the Southern Hemisphere. (It was eclipsed by the 641-yard 2nd hole at the Gary Player Country Club, in Sun City, South Africa.)

Framing the fairways is a freckled forest of tamarind, *mukwa*, and vase-shape *mopani* alive with fork-tailed *drongos*, crimson-breasted bush shrike, and carmine bee-eaters, their red and turquoise feathers brilliant in the sun. During the long African summer, sharp-eyed golfers often sight the diedrik cuckoo, a robin-size bird with a deep-emerald-colored back and a black bill. "*Dee-dee-dee-deeder-ick!*" screams the male with brain-shredding force. "*Deea-deaa-deea!*" answers the female over the shushing of golfers on the green.

Hippo footprints are most often found on holes six and seven. Though the club has no record of a golfer being mashed underfoot, Sihole recommends staying out of their paths. Hippos are supposed to account for more deaths in Africa than any other creature (except mosquitoes). Only one golfer has been killed by a hippo at Konkola, and he was in a car. His Toyota blindsided a female emerging from the bush. Both died on impact.

Among the mourners was the hippo's mate, a reticent night crawler nicknamed Elliott. By day, Elliott hides beneath the Nile cabbage that chokes the pond off hole eight. Normally, the only things you can see moving in the lush vegetation are kingfishers and squacco herons. But sometimes Elliott peeks above the cabbage to ponder the play of a passing foursome. "We're proud of Elliott," says Trish Houston. "He's not a golfer, but he seems to take an interest in the game." Beneath a waning sun and matted clouds, Sihole, Musopelo, and I engage in some fairway one-downsmanship. Sihole says the most hazardous course he ever played was near Mutare, in neighboring Zimbabwe. During the 1970s, when that country was at war, the rules at the Hillside Golf Club allowed a free drop if a golfer's ball landed in a crater left by mortar fire.

"Paradise!" grumbles Musopelo, citing another Zimbabwean course, in Centenary, where players were permitted to repeat a shot if their swing was interrupted by gunfire or explosions, and they were advised to check for land mines before putting.

"A walk in the park!" I sniff, and trump them both. "The 1976 Victoria Falls Classic had snipers in the bunkers."

"Perhaps that is how bunkers got their name," cracks Sihole.

As the sweet scent of Natal mahogany mingles with smoke from distant brushfires, Sihole plucks a 3-wood from his bag and hands it to Musopelo. "Land a ball in the middle of the pond," Sihole says, "and I'll give you a million kwacha."

Musopelo grins broadly. "If I do," he says, "and you swim out to get it, you can have the million back."

There's something enigmatic and prehistoric about crocodiles, as if he were designed by a committee of paleontologists. The ones at Konkola appear to be silvery rocks on the bank until they glide into the water. The caddies call the largest Inywena. That's "big croc" in Bemba, the lingua franca of the Copperbelt. Inywena appears to be about 13 feet from tail to snout. He would have been even longer, but something chomped a foot or two off his tail. It may have been Inywena himself.

Crocodiles are given to nibbling on their tails, especially when hungry. But then crocs eat practically anything. The contents of the stomach of a crocodile shot in Botswana's Okavango Swamp in 1968 included the remains of a zebra, a donkey, two goats, and the still-clothed torso of a woman who had been missing 17 days. Adult crocs have no real natural enemies except humans, possibly because they're meaner.

Crocodiles used to polish off as many as 20,000 Africans a year. They still average about one a week in Zambia. A single crocodile is said to have killed 400 people—a croc hardly matters in Africa until it has eaten a half dozen or so. Still, despite its appetite for humans, the crocodile's chief diet at Konkola is fish and the occasional puppy.

After Inywena sinks into the drink, I slink off and order a beer, with caterpillars on the side. After a few brews, the grubs seem almost palatable. I ask barman Laswell Luhana, who has worked at Konkola since 1963, how many golfers the club has lost to crocs. "They haven't taken anyone," he reports, "though they've damaged a few." Four caddies, two thieves.

"One thief was fishing, with the police looking for him," Luhana says, "but the croc caught him." The thief made off with copper; the croc, a leg.

A few years ago, a golfer offered his caddy the equivalent of 8 cents to comb a pond for an errant shot. As the caddy poked around in the murky, green water, a submerged croc chomped on his backside. Fortunately, he escaped with only minor lacerations. "You forget about the crocodiles," says Nkandu, the pro at Ndola. "If you try to be a bit courageous, definitely, they come for you."

But the most harrowing encounter with a Konkola croc occurred on November 6, 1981. The play-by-play was recounted in the local Mining Mirror under the headline SCREAMS...... THEN RESCUE AT GOLF COURSE: CADDY NEARLY MAULED TO DEATH.

According to an eyewitness account, four golfers on the first green heard cries of "*nafwaa ee*" ("I am dying") coming from the pond off the ninth fairway. The golfers and their caddies ran through the rough. To their horror, a croc was dragging the screaming caddy into deeper water. One of the foursome recalled, "We stood there flabbergasted and dumbfounded to see a human being dragged to be eaten alive by this ugly-looking monster."

A golfer and a caddy waded into the water and grabbed the screaming caddy by his shoulders. "We started pulling the victim from the crocodile, which had bitten and had clang [sic] to his right arm," said the golfer. "As we pulled away hard, the victim's arm snapped like a dry twig in the crocodile's mouth and broke."

The croc stopped "clanging." When they finally yanked the caddy ashore, the croc charged and snagged the caddy's buttocks. The golfer kept the beast at bay with his putter. After a while it let go, turned, and slithered back into the pond. Doctors severed the caddy's right arm. He now makes a slender living selling cigarettes at the Kitwe bus station.

Occasionally, even a player is confronted by a croc in this heart of golfness. Over Zambeers and caterpillars at Konkola's 19th hole, Sihole tells a tale through Inywena eyes. Call it *Guess Who's Coming as Dinner*.

"The golfer, he looks so *tasty*," Sihole says, crunching on a caterpillar for effect. "He sees me and he runs away very fast. I see this tasty golfer and run toward him very, very fast."

Musopelo takes a big swig of the Zambrew and says, "The golfer's partner rescued him." Musopelo takes a bigger swig. "He dispatched the reptile with a blow to the head."

As every Konkola member knows, the course can chew you up—and it swallows.

PING!

LA HABRA, CALIFORNIA

David.

"If we ever have a boy, let's name him after David Pureifory of the Green Bay Packers," Da-i Ping remembers telling his wife, Julie. "He's fierce and tenacious." Which is how the Chinese-born jujitsu master, who had helped the defensive lineman rehab a serious knee injury, chose a name for his only son.

Ping.

"I've got a name for my putter," Karsten Solheim exclaimed to his wife, Louise. "Listen to it *ping*." Which is how the Norwegian-born mechanical engineer, who had been tinkering with the club in his garage, chose a name for his golf equipment company.

David Ping.

Until 2005, the name, full of sound and fury, signified nothing in professional golf. Having turned pro on a lark after qualifying for the 2001 Buick Open, Ping stumbled through the low minors with one measly victory to show for it, at something called the IGTA Orlando Classic in 2003. First place at the mini-mini tour event was worth $10,000—ensuring that, for one week at least, Ping would break even. Normally, he didn't. In 2004, he shelled out $70,000 pursuing bush league golf and took in only $15,000.

"Basically, my wife Karen and I lived off her salary," says the 30-year-old Ping. Karen made a modest—very modest—income as a first-grade teacher at Ocean View Elementary in Whittier, California. The couple shared a tiny—very tiny—condo in La Habra that was scrunched into a development off South Beach Boulevard, about 20 miles from an actual beach. "David couldn't carry a second job," says his father, now a prominent sports agent. "You can't improve your game playing part-time."

By the spring of 2005, David and Karen had $7.53 in the bank and a debt of $140,000—the result of loans, tournament entrance fees, travel expenses, and nine maxed-out credit cards. To make things worse, Ping's sponsor, Slippers International, had given him the slip and dropped him. "All our friends and relatives knew we were struggling," he says, "but none of them knew how much."

So much, it turns out, that it had become a weekly ritual for Karen to phone her husband after a rough opening round and beg him to "shoot a 66" so he would make the cut and they could pay the rent. More often than not he'd shoot a 67 or a 68: From the winter of 2004 to the spring of 2005, Ping missed 12 cuts by a stroke or two. "You can only take so many doors getting slammed in your face before you start second-guessing yourself," he says. "I got to the point where I just wanted to puke on myself."

By the end of that April, Ping says he was just a few weeks away from quitting the Small Time and becoming a glass salesman. "The worst nightmare of any golfer who dreams about joining the PGA Tour is knowing you have to go back to a nine-to-five job," Ping says. His dream was becoming that nightmare.

All that changed on May 11, when fortune smiled—broadly and unexpectedly—on Ping and his partner Garth Mulroy at the inaugural Big Stakes Match Play in Mesquite, Nevada. Ping and Mulroy, a 26-year-old South African who had qualified for only a handful of Nationwide Tour events, survived the first five rounds. Then they beat club pros Rick Martmann and Mark Mielke 2-up in the final.

It was a lovely TV moment for a journeyman who hadn't been good enough to make the roster on either the Coastal Carolina or University of Michigan teams. The winner's take was $3 million, the richest ever in golf. "A week later a check for the entire amount arrived at my apartment in California," Ping recalls. "Talk about surreal: I actually prayed to God that the check would clear." Thankfully, it did. After giving Mulroy his share and paying off their backers—NFL offensive linemen Barry Stokes and Ross Burba—Ping pocketed $725,000, settled his finances and forgot about selling glass.

Since then, his life seems to have gone through a curious period of suspension, like those cartoon characters who go on running horizontally off the edge of a cliff until eventually they plummet. "We haven't changed our lifestyles and we're not eating at fancier restaurants," says Ping. He and Karen did move to Omaha to run her father's hardware business. "We're trying to be smart with our money. We want to be the same ordinary people we were before all this happened to us."

Ping is disarmingly ordinary, a personality who would melt into any crowd, a player with negligible talent, but the owner of inviolable determination. "I've always believed in my dream," he says. "And the dream is playing my heart out until I make the PGA."

These days, everyone he knows (and some he doesn't) seems to want to dream for him. Friends, relatives, and the most casual of acquaintances feel compelled to tell him how to peel out his billfold. A member of his old country club took him aside at a gathering and counseled: "I'm just going to tell you one thing: The best investment you could make would be to buy a home in Southern California."

A few minutes later, another member cornered him and said: "Just don't buy a house in Southern California. It's the worst investment you could make."

Ping smiled and introduced the two real estate experts. As they argued the merits of the market, Ping slunk away. "When I left the club those two were still debating," he says. "The minute someone tries to sell me something, I hit the door and run as fast as I can."

Still, he must have bought *somebody's* sales pitch: After all, he pumped cash into five oil wells and six natural gas lines in Tennessee and Kentucky. "I had people go out and confirm that the sites actually exist," he says, sheepishly. "As long as the ventures are successful, Karen and I don't care if gas prices go up."

Perhaps the sagest investment advice was offered by Stokes, the Atlanta Falcon who fronted Ping half his $100,000 Big Stakes entry fee. "I told David to buy himself a present, like a car, and put the rest away," Stokes says. "You've got to congratulate yourself, right?"

Ping had been perfectly content tooling from tournament to tournament in his 2000 Volkswagen Jetta, the one with 140,000 miles on the odometer. "I told Karen I could drive it another 100,000 miles," he says. "She thought that was a great idea until she took the wheel and the engine started cutting out. That's when she demanded that I get new wheels." So he sprang for a BMW 330i (retail price: $36,300).

Mulroy—who invested most of his loot in stocks and bonds—bought a Mercedes C55 AMG ($55,225). "Then Garth rubbed it in my face," Ping cracks. "Maybe greed got to him." Mulroy struggled on the Nationwide Tour in 2006 (he pocketed all of $4,195), but had a respectable 2007, making 20 cuts and $146,272.

Ping barely finished in the money after the Big Stakes. Competing on a sponsor's exemption at the Buick Open in 2005, he shot a 77 and a 75 to miss the cut by 12 strokes. He also left empty-handed at three Nationwide events: the Cleveland Open, the Cox Classic in Omaha, and the Envirocore Utah Classic. The next year he entered four Nation-wide tournaments and left with $1,167. "I just have to stay humble and work with what I've got," says Ping. What he *lacks* at the moment is a consistent long game.

"David fully realizes he's not PGA Tour material," says Andy Thuney, head pro at Hacienda. "He's good, but not great, and now he knows what it's like to go up against the heavy hitters. The truth is he needs a partner to play well. If he's going to make a living in the sport, it's got to be in events like the Big Stakes."

A financial bust in 2005, the Big Stakes went belly-up in 2006. The event was revived in 2007 and relocated to Las Vegas. Alas, Ping and his new partner lost their second-round qualifier and returned home without even a little stake. "David can quit and become a club pro like the rest of us shlubs," Thuney says. "Here's the dilemma: After hitting the big jackpot, should he walk away and say, 'Hey, I got lucky' and cash out? Or should he keep returning to the tables and possibly squander what was a godsend? The problem is that we've all got the soul of a gambler in us."

Ping says his dream cannot be deferred. "It's never been about winning one big tournament," he protests. "It's about making my card."

Whether Ping ultimately dreams on or dreams off, his wife is happy just to be free of creditors. "The best part of all," Karen says, "is that I didn't have to teach summer school."

DOGGING IT

SANTA ROSA, CALIFORNIA

Charlie Brown: "I have a new philosophy : Life is like a golf course."
Snoopy: "And a sand trap runs through it."

One morning when Charles Schulz was a boy, he and his buddies rode their bikes to a golf course in St. Paul. "It was about five o'clock," he remembered years later, "and we were the only ones there." If desire had anything to do with talent, they would have been pretty good, but their clubs were old and miserable. Schulz chunked and chunked and shot 156. He thought, Next week we'll come here again and I'll be better. And they did come the next week. And Schulz chunked and chunked and shot 165. "I was a terrible failure," Schulz once told me. "My play was embarrassing, agonizing. It was as if I were in a bad dream."

Schulz was an enormously successful cartoonist given over to dreaminess and painful introspection. When he died in 2000, at age 77, he had drawn *Peanuts* for almost 50 years, and his pen-and-ink duffers were still shooting 156, 165, and 234. *Peanuts* was a child's garden of reverses, set in an eternal suburb where kids shared the disillusion of the grown-up world yet refused to grow up themselves. Schulz's strips were full of nimble sagacity, coppery melancholy, and a golf-playing beagle.

Like Charlie Brown, his most famous character, Schulz had an easy face and soft eyes that radiated humility and self-doubt. He spoke with gentle humor, quoting his characters' warm, chuckly aphorisms as if they'd been uttered by real people. "Charlie Brown once told Snoopy he found it strange that the golfing gods had never allowed him to make a hole-in-one," Schulz would say mildly. "When he asked Snoopy what that meant, Snoopy replied, 'It means we need some new golfing gods.'"

Golf was arguably the biggest thing in Schulz's world, and sports may have been the biggest thing in Charlie Brown's. Certainly it accounted for some of *Peanuts'* undying popularity. Season after season, Charlie Brown took the mound bursting with pride and hope; year after year, Lucy smirkingly yanked the football away just as he was about to kick it. Charlie Brown was never a golfer. "He's a caddy," Schulz explained. "He caddies for Snoopy because there's more money in it."

Sports allowed Schulz to move freely from childish games to adult concerns. They provided him with an easy way to express frustration. He often twisted sports clichés to make all sorts of little commentaries on life. "Winning isn't everything," Linus says consolingly.

"But losing isn't *anything*," answers Charlie Brown.

Losing, in fact, was *Peanuts* in a nutshell. "Winning is happy," noted Schulz, "but happy isn't funny."

A theologian once observed that Charlie Brown's pose on the pitcher's mound is not unlike that of Job on the ash heap. Schulz didn't dismiss the parallel, but he didn't dwell on it, either. He said simply that he liked the contemplative quality of baseball, of a pitcher rubbing the ball with two out and the bases loaded in the bottom of the ninth.

Schulz himself had a sad and sentimental way of looking at the most innocuous event. Take, for instance, a PGA tournament on TV. A golfer blows a huge lead on the final hole; the camera pans across the stunned faces in the crowd and zooms in on him. "I think, This guy has to go back to a lonely hotel room and brood about losing," Schulz said. "How can he stand it? It bothers me. It's ridiculous, of course, but it bothers me."

How could Charlie Brown stand it? He was an eternal victim whose efforts to raise his team to respectability were doomed from the start. He never won, he never even *expected* to win, but he was not reconciled to losing. "How can we," he asked, "when we're so sincere?" Even the one time Charlie Brown's team won, it had to forfeit its victory because its shortstop, Snoopy, bet a nickel on the other team.

But even in defeat, Charlie Brown was not defeated. He remained unbowed. "Rats!" he said. "I can't stand it." And he trudged back to the mound.

"What's the sense in our playing when we know we're going to lose?" asked Lucy. "If there was even a million-to-one chance we might win, it would make some sense."

"Well," replied Charlie Brown, "there may not be a million-to-one chance, but I'm sure there's at least a billion-to-one chance."

If Charlie Brown ever did win, said Schulz, he wouldn't be Charlie Brown. "It would be like John McEnroe's suddenly being a nice guy instead of constantly disgracing himself," he said. "You can't destroy your basic premise."

So his hero remained a schlemiel Sisyphus. He pushed on despite the apathy and ridicule of his teammates, making do on a combination of woebegone innocence and baffled optimism. One April Fools' Day, the treacherous Lucy told him Ted Williams was at the front door. She said he wanted advice on how to manage a baseball team. In the end, Charlie Brown stood alone on the doorstep, saying, "It could have happened."

Lucy was his constant tormentor. When she pulled the annual placekicking stunt, she grinned like a very pleased pumpkin. Tumbling through the air, Charlie Brown wore a wry, wounded look. It was Ronald Reagan's favorite *Peanuts* shtick.

"These children affect us because in a certain sense they are monsters," wrote the novelist Umberto Eco, a professor of semiotics at the University of Bologna. "They are the monstrous infantile reductions of all the neuroses of a modern citizen of industrial civilization."

Such rococo appraisals aside, Schulz did tend to see kids as little monsters, though he had five of his own. Originally, he intended *Peanuts* to depict the battle for dominance in the playground; his very first strip showed the harsh cruelty kids can inflict on one another, and it did so without the leavening of humor he developed later. "Well! Here comes ol Charlie Brown," says a kid sitting on a curb. "Good ol Charlie Brown . . . How I hate him!"

"A lot of adults forget how difficult it is to be a child," said Schulz, who at 77 still remembered an incident some 65 years before when a playmate got slam-dunked in the face with a football. "I've always despised bullies. They never let us play totally at peace. They made the playgrounds dangerous."

Actually, Minnesota wasn't all that barbarous a place in the '20s and '30s, and Schulz grew up in a benignly innocent setting. His father was a barber who didn't have time for sports. Sometimes he would take his son to Mille Lacs Lake to fish. Schulz hated it. "I've done Snoopy fishing," he allowed, "but the worms always attack his friend Woodstock and tie him to a tree."

Hockey he learned by swatting tennis balls at his grandmother while she gamely tended goal in the basement with a broom. "I like to think she made a lot of great saves," he said wistfully. Schulz liked hockey, loved golf. "You always had to try out for other sports," he recalled. "With baseball and hockey, there was always a coach to say that you weren't good enough. But golf, you were on your own, and you didn't have to be part of another team. It was just you, and that was it. And that was a great revelation."

For a couple of years Schulz looped at the Highland Park course, where, in the late 1940s, he captured the caddy championship. "Last thing I ever won," he said. "Back then the caddy rate was 75 cents, and I never got more than a 25 cent tip."

Peppermint Patty: "I think this putt breaks to the right, Marcie ... "
Marcie: "It goes left, sir."
Peppermint Patty: "I think it's slightly uphill, Marcie ... "
Marcie: "It's downhill, sir."
Peppermint Patty: "It's gonna go in, Marcie!"
Marcie: "It's gonna miss, sir."
Peppermint Patty: "What kind of caddy are you, Marcie?!"
Marcie: "Typical, sir."

Schulz had mastered the game by chipping tennis balls to his black-and-white pointer, Spike, with an old 9-iron. Spike, a gifted dog who fetched potatoes from the cellar on command, was the subject of a sketch Schulz sent to *Ripley's Believe It or Not* with the caption: "A hunting dog that eats pins, tacks, and razor blades." It was his first published drawing. Eventually, Spike became the inspiration for

Schulz's best-loved creation, Charlie Brown's irrepressibly waggish beagle.

Unlike his master, Snoopy was more wishy than washy. From atop his doghouse he led an elaborate fantasy life that often found him competing in the Masters or on Centre Court at Wimbledon. But when he climbed down, he could be a hot dog too, starting double plays by snaring grounders in his teeth and spitting them to the second baseman.

Snoopy was perhaps the worst sport in *Peanuts,* a trait that helped to keep him human. When Charlie Brown asked him what his handicap was, Snoopy replied, "I'm a scratch golfer. I write down all my good scores and scratch out all my bad ones." In tennis, after a double fault, he smashed, wanged, booted, stomped, whapped, and crunched his racket into the court. Then he sat down at his typewriter and tapped out: "Gentlemen: Under separate cover I am returning a defective tennis racket." At the rink, he took advantage of the national anthem to score three goals.

Schulz played his hockey in the streets. He and his friends would wait until the snowplows had come through and then scrape off the loose snow to expose the icy road surface. They'd pile clumps of snow at either end of the block to mark the goals. Male drivers would always slow down and weave around the goalposts, claimed Schulz, but women would roll right over them. "The men knew how important those clumps were to us," he said. "But the women just didn't understand."

Neither did Lucy, Charlie Brown's indifferent outfielder. Fly balls always dropped in gentle arcs five feet behind her. "What in the world made you miss that one?" screamed Charlie Brown.

"I was having my quiet time," she said.

Young Schulz was as devoted to golf as Charlie Brown was to baseball. He would show up at the St. Paul Open at dawn and spend the entire day shadowing golfers. Just as Charlie Brown worshipped the hapless Joe Shlabotnick of the lowly Green Grass League, Schulz's hero was Ralph Guldahl, a two-time winner of the National Open. "I was the only soldier in Ralph's army," Schulz said. "I remember him looking at me once wondering, Who's this kid following me around? He's the only one here."

As a teenager, he latched onto the great Sam Snead. Schulz never forgot the day he walked into the sporting goods section of a St. Paul department store and spotted a set of Sam Snead irons. "That was the most beautiful thing I had ever seen in my life," he said, "but they cost $100, and there was no way in the world I could have afforded them." He died still wishing he'd owned the set.

Schulz knew the strange symptoms of golf fever and the incurable longings associated with it. "Golf is like women," he said. "Golf leads us on. You hit a perfect drive. You hit the 3-wood right up there near the green, and you're thinking birdie all the way up there, and then you chunk the approach shot and you get a bogey or a double bogey. So you've been led on, and then you're turned down again. I suppose that's the fascination of the game, but that's the most aggravating part of it too."

Nearly all of Schulz's early sketches were spurned; his

cartoons were even rejected by the editors of his high school yearbook. It wasn't until Schulz had been to war and taught a correspondence course in art that he published his first panel. It ran in a magazine called *Timeless Topix*, and the caption said, "Judy, if your batting average was just a little higher, I think I could really fall in love with you."

Schulz's strips were syndicated in more than 2,000 newspapers around the world, and his characters appeared on everything from lunch pails to electronic games. He had no assistants: He drew every panel and inked in every word balloon. "Arnie Palmer doesn't have another golfer hit his 9-iron for him," he explained. "He does it all. I do it all. He has a caddy. Of course, I don't even have a caddy."

Schulz lived simply, his one indulgence the indoor ice rink across the street from his studio in Santa Rosa. He built the arena in 1970 and ran it, at a loss, as a sort of philanthropic hobby. He organized a bunch of youth hockey leagues, with the provision that every kid who came out got to play, and for a long time, he refereed games himself. "I took great satisfaction in protecting everybody and making sure all the calls were right," he said, sounding like the catcher in the rye. "And yet all I ever got was criticism." He was abused by the players, who slashed him, fans who spat at him, and parents who yelled, "Hey, Schulz, we can't win because it's your arena." So he retired from reffing.

He complained frequently about the hypocrisy of the grown-up world, but adults never appeared in *Peanuts*. The reason, Schulz said, was that they would intrude. "We live in a society of angry people," he said. "That's why they go to games, take their shirts off, drink 30 beers, and yell, 'We're Number One.' "

At golf pro-ams, he tended to stay out of galleries, and though he routinely shot in the high 70s in his low 70s, he avoided competing in front of large crowds. "Sparky's anxiety was often high," says onetime pro Mac O'Grady. "He'd be afraid he'd look silly or shank the ball and hurt somebody. One year at the Crosby, he was so nervous, he wouldn't play."

Charlie Brown: "Tournament golf can be very nerve-wracking. Do you get nervous when you're on the first tee?"
Snoopy: "I don't know ... I've never made it to the first tee."

Schulz used to worry that while his characters were developing, he was winding down. "My drives off the tee used to be a lot longer," he lamented at age 73. "I used to be a good putter. Now my hands aren't as steady, so my putting is falling apart little by little." In the early 1980s, while playing slo-pitch, he misjudged a routine fly ball and watched it sail over his head. "I always prided myself on being a good fielder," he said. "It was so humiliating to have reached the age where I'd lost the knack of knowing where the ball was. It was my first realization that I was suddenly an old man."

"I used to be able to dodge those line drives," Charlie Brown told Lucy after getting beaned by a batted ball.

"When you get old," she said, "your reflexes slow down." Still, at age 72, Schulz achieved a lifelong goal of every golfer—one that Charlie Brown wouldn't dare to dream: He got a hole-in-one.

Schulz was competitive about his strip until the very end. He paid close attention to the various polls that were supposed to determine which comic strip was the most popular. "Once you get caught up in them, you're running in a race," he said. "It's nice to be on top, but when I don't come in first, I can rationalize it.

"I suppose it's like being an old athlete. It's a thrill to put on the Yankee uniform when you're a rookie, but when you've been putting it on for 15 years, it gets to be old hat. Your ambitions change. You get old so fast, and as the world begins to open up, you ask yourself, Has it been worth it to be at the drawing board day after day doing cartoons?"

"Cartooning is not glamorous or important, but I've made it look like it is. I wonder if my ambition was a little misguided. But what else could I have done?"

All that soul-searching had its consolations. "Charlie Brown said, 'Life is full of choices, but you never get any.' I'd dearly love to have won the U.S. Amateur or the World Series, but what I've done, I think, is much better."

Schulz left one small golf legacy. Near the start of the millennium, a large fairway bunker at his old St. Paul course was reshaped into the outline of Snoopy. Happily ever after, one hopes, the 15th hole will feature more than a dogleg. It has the whole dog.

THE STAR OF DAVID

AMELIA ISLAND, FLORIDA

For most of us working stiffs, going on a corporate outing is like being fed intravenously: You never taste anything, but eventually you feel a kind of ghostly satiation. But if you're a golf nut, the chance to schmooze with a fairway legend can turn just another company retreat into something as memorable as your first backdoor.

Many pros make a tidy living spending their Mondays and Tuesdays mixing business people with the game of golf. The work is easy, the pay borders on the obscene. You blow into town in the morning, give a clinic, and in the afternoon, play a hole or two with each group. If the guest list is too big, you camp out at a par 3 and hit tee shots with every foursome that comes through. You wrap things up by mingling at a cocktail party and handing out booby prizes at a dinner, after which you regale people with tales of Arnold and Jack and Tiger. If you're a hit, everyone goes home inspired and maybe shaves a stroke or two off their handicaps.

The original king of corporate outings is Dave Stockton, winner of the 1970 and 1976 PGA Championships. He appeared in more than 90 in some years and, before scaling down his schedule a decade ago, reportedly earned in excess of $600,000 in ancillary loot. A sober speaker, Stockton expounds on the minutiae of the sport.

The reigning clown prince of the corporate grind is David Feherty, the gently subversive CBS golf commentator. His all-day deal features photo ops, benign dish on tour players, and an inexhaustible fund of gratuitous insults. "I basically get paid to be a smart-ass show-off," says the onetime Ryder Cup player. "Golfers think that if I rip their game, it goes to a higher level. Well, maybe. It still looks pretty low to me." For such bunker sniping, Feherty gets from $20,000 to $25,000 a day, plus expenses.

He plays about two dozen corporate gigs a year. "I'm really just a B-list celebrity," he says. "No one knows what I took like. I'm just a voice." A relaxed, unpretentious, word-caressing voice that flows over listeners like an eruption in a caramel factory. "You know why I like talking to corporate America," he purrs. "It looks good on a parole application."

THE AIRPORT

Early one morning not long ago, Feherty left home, family, and parole board behind in Dallas to attend an outing at the Golf Club in Amelia Island, Florida. He'd been hired by a security outfit that manufactures Mace and body armor. In the baggage area at the Jacksonville Airport, Feherty's face is glazed with the unmistakable blankness that occurs when one week's company retreat blends with the previous week's—an expression not unlike the one my youngest daughter had midway through our mini golf marathon in Chapter 13. He is puzzled by the absence of a limo driver brandishing a sign with his name—or a semblance of it.

He ticks off about a dozen of the variations he has sighted in the mitts of limo drivers: FEHERITY, FERRITY, FEHRRITY, FLAHERTY, FLERITY ... "It gets closer and closer to O'Fleritty, the original Gaelic," he says. "I don't know how that transformed into Feherty—some ancestor must have married a Protestant or slept with a sheep."

THE CLINIC

Most business people who meet Feherty conclude, fairly quickly, that he is mad. "In reality, I'm not," he says. "In reality, I'm a miserable bastard, but people actually seem to enjoy that."

In reality, Feherty is friendly, approachable, a mischievous soul who delights in the company of others and in all things scatological. On this particular morning, standing on a putting green surrounded by 52 Mace-makers, he watches a hacker popcorn a tee shot into deep rough. "That drive was like a giraffe's ass," he says. "High and smelly."

He's wearing a short-sleeve shirt, green linen shorts, and open-toe sandals. "Isn't this the sort of lovely morning that makes you glad to be alive?" asks Feherty. "The only way you could ruin a day like today is to play golf on it."

It's hard to imagine anyone in the world ever disliking Feherty, but two years ago a woman did slug him at a bank outing in Wisconsin. "This lady took exception to me taking exception to Martha Burk's crusade against the men-only policy at Augusta National," he says. "I told the lady I would have hit her back but I didn't want my ass kicked. She was not only bigger than me, but on the Anheuser side of Busch."

A doughy duffer asks: "Did the punch hurt your game?"

"If I'd had a game," says Feherty, "it certainly would have."

Feherty takes a half-dozen chip shots to the 18th hole, about 60 yards away. The last one lands about two feet from the flag.

"You look great," says a security guy.

"Thank you," says Feherty. "You're a very attractive man yourself."

Doughy duffer: "What's it like to cover the Masters?"

Feherty: "Every time I climb into my broadcast tower on the 16th hole, I feel like I'm in a gay bar in a hospital gown. I want to sit down quickly and say as little as possible"

Stockton, the corporate king, preaches the heavy-mental game. Feherty comes off less as preacher than as repentant sinner. "When I was a pro, anytime I played great, I had it set in my mind that I was going to accept the consequences," Feherty says. "That's the best advice I can give. It stinks, but that's all I've got. Ninety percent of the time, this game is a nightmare—you're either topping the ball or sending it into the trees. But the feeling you get after hitting a shot right is the closest you can get to a sporting orgasm."

He imparts a few words of wisdom about shanking ("The easiest shot to hit by accident and the hardest to hit on purpose") and the sand wedge. "You may think I'm gonna change your game," he tells the throng, "but it's more likely I'll just screw it up. No matter what I do here or what I show you, by the time I'm done, you're still going to suck."

THE FAIRWAY MINGLE

Given three hours to mix with 13 groups of golfers, Feherty wheels around the course as if he were in the last lap of the Indy 500 time trials with an hour to make up. "I've done 32 groups over this amount of time," he says. "I felt like I was in a drive-by. After a while, you run out of cheerfulness, and your attitude turns to pure evil. It's like, Just write the check!"

For now, Feherty is brimming with bonhomie. A man in a shirt that seems cut from an early cubist canvas asks him for his opinion of on-air sidekick Gary McCord. "It's like working with a chimp," he says, then tries to soften to the blow: "I mean, a chimp who plays golf very well."

Feherty takes wicked pleasure in knocking others. "I can't affect anybody's game, really," he says. "I mean, not on one hole. I'm not going to significantly affect anybody's life, so I might as well screw with them. I love watching people suffer as long as they don't get hurt. Badly."

Today's golfers are suffering, all right. The fairways are abuzz with banana balls and blade shots and chili dips.

"Let's see what you've got," Feherty tells a man so large he has his own field of gravity.

Gravity Man whiffs.

"Not much," says Feherty.

Gravity Man whiffs again. "I'm terrible," he says.

"Don't talk yourself down," Feherty says in a soothing tone. "That's my job."

He pulls up beside a threesome whose mouths are only slightly filthier than their FootJoys. One tells a joke about a pedophile; the second, a prisoner; the third, Brad Pitt. Feherty tops them all with one about two Irishmen and a sausage.

Prison Joker wants to know how to prevent a slice. Feherty advises him to close his stance. He inches his lead foot toward the ball, takes a quivering swing, and holes out. "Very nice shot without method," says Feherty. "Everything moved but your bowels, and the jury's out on that."

Everyone laughs. "Okay," says Feherty, "I've diminished your self-esteem enough. And I've seen enough golf, or whatever that was."

Just as he's about to drive off, his cell phone rings. "Honey, I parked my truck at the airport," Feherty says. "Sorry I didn't say goodbye before I left … I didn't want to wake you … I love you too." He hangs up. "In case you were wondering," he tells the jokers, "that was McCord."

THE COCKTAIL HOUR

It's said that a life of complete self-indulgence, if led with the whole heart, may also bring wisdom. Feherty, whose beverage of choice has always been Bushmills Irish Whiskey, found the palace of wisdom a chilly place. He quit drinking—cold turkey—in January, 2005. "I'd become a bloated half-man, half-mattress," he tells a woman at the courtyard reception. "My kids actually used me as furniture."

Nonetheless, the reputation of hell-raiser clings to him like a fly to butter. When offered a highball, he politely declines. "It's amazing what happens when you're sober at midnight," he explains. "You actually go to bed."

Unlike most recovering lushes, he steadfastly refuses to repent his former ways. On the contrary, he remembers them with huge affection. "I was the Tiger Woods of drinking: I consumed a bottle and a half a day," he tells a member of the catering crew. "My liver was so shot that I actually asked Pat Summerall for his old one."

Did you ever think of getting help?

"No, I could drink it all by myself." *Ba-dum-bum.*

After turning down liquor for an hour, he tries a different tack. "Actually, I'm on reverse 'roids," he tells a well-oiled guest. "I bulked down and lost 50 pounds. On the bright side, my testicles are *huge*."

DINNER AND THE SPEECH

Feherty has a rule about food at outings: If it looks like it should be in a Kleenex, he won't eat it. He doesn't touch his crab cake.

As dessert is served, he's called to the podium to hand out prizes for the most balls lost, the coldest putter, and the longest club toss. He retells the joke about the two Irishmen and the sausage. He retails stories about the notoriously tight Nick Faldo ("He wakes up in the middle of the night to make sure he hasn't lost any sleep"), slow-witted broadcaster David Clampett ("I told David, 'Never start a sentence with 'Lannie, I think … '—because you don't"), and Woods ("Will Tiger ever smile again? I imagine he does every night").

He rules the room for a good 30 minutes and steps off to loud applause. Gravity Man shouts: "I want to be you when I grow up."

Feherty shakes his head. "If you grow up," he says, "you can't be me."

ICE CAPADES

LECONTE BAY, ALASKA

There's nothing quite as chilling as an iceberg. Especially if you're kayaking through Alaska's Inside Passage before the steep, towering face of LeConte Glacier. LeConte is like some great living thing that for 15,000 years has calved ice into the sea in huge, frightening chunks. The crumbling glacier fills the bay with bergs and floes that get as big as the White House.

There's nothing quite as cool as an ice floe. Especially if you're dodging one in the murky waters of LeConte Bay. The shifting seascape of ice can leave a kayaker as giddy as an 8-year-old finding shapes in clouds. Sort out the jagged images, and you'll see the wonders of the ancient world: a pyramid, a Sphinx, godlike figures. You keep waiting for the Hanging Gardens of Babylon.

It was my own 8-year-old who got me hot over ice. Daisy had been reading about baidarkas, the primitive kayaks in which the Aleuts once ranged the ice fields. One morning around our Pennsylvania breakfast table, she said: "I want to go to Alaska and paddle a kayak and see a salmon." The only negotiable part was the salmon. Daisy would settle for a woolly mammoth embedded in ice, or possibly Sasquatch.

My reason for going involved a different sort of ice capade. I was hoping to try my hand at glacial golf, a variation on the game played on pack ice in Greenland. Ice golf is quite similar to the traditional game, apart from the fact that the green is white, the balls are purple, and the golfer's fingers, blue. And of course, the doglegs tend to belong to huskies.

So one summer day, Daisy, my father-in-law, and I headed to Alaska for five days of camping and sea-kayaking. We signed on with an outfitter with trips up and down the 49th state. We chose down: LeConte is the southernmost active tidewater glacier in the northern hemisphere.

Like all freshwater glaciers, LeConte empties into salt-water. The chunks break into floes that ply the bay, menacing kayakers like pirate galleys. An awesome armada drifts heavily out to Frederick Sound—some with luminous white masts, others with hulls glowing in colors found only in 128-packs of Crayolas. Those with slick, glassy flanks have recently capsized, as icebergs do when they slowly melt underwater and grow lopsided.

The possibility of getting flipped into 37 degree waters rules out climbing aboard a berg. Which disappoints Daisy. She had planned to have a tea party on one with her stuffed wolf, Claudius. But Daisy is cheered by the spectacle of white ice on green water. "It looks like marshmallows dancing in mint tea," she observes.

Our 10-member, six-kayak expedition picks its way through popweed and sea kelp. I'm the helmsman of a two-hole kayak, steering by means of a foot-controlled rudder in the stern. Daisy and my father-in-law take turns in the bow. My father-in-law, a onetime second petty officer on the *U.S.S. Missouri*, navigates as if he has just sighted a rogue iceberg from the deck of the Titanic. "Dodge that ice, dammit!" he shouts. "Watch out, for crissake!" I say I'm having trouble keeping my bumper-car instincts in check. He says that's not how exploring works; you're supposed to survive so you can tell of your adventures.

Daisy is more intrepid. "Ice at 12 o'clock," she yells. "Full speed ahead." To her ice is nice, but bumping is better. "I feel like I'm blindfolded in a spook house," she says. The bergs creak and moan and crackle in counterpoint to the long, burry whistles of the varied thrush and the high, tinkling trills of the winter wren. A covey of eagles wheels overhead, and seals and sea otters pop their heads up from the water to stare at us quizzically. Convinced the otters they hunted were transformed humans, the Aleuts tried to lure them by wearing festive gutskin raincoats and wooden-peaked hats. Daisy is decked out in a far less stylish jumpsuit of polypropylene, the material that accounts for the recent sea-kayaking boom. It allows you to paddle around glaciers without becoming one.

With the mercury nudging 20, Daisy dons her ice togs for a late-afternoon round of glacier golf. Our guides have set up a five-hole pitch and putt course on the shore. The holes are sections of PVC pipe hammered into the snow; the flagstaffs, plastic grocery bags tied to paddles; the obstacles, a herd of beached bergs jutting out of the tundra. "How do you plan to hit over *them*?" asks Daisy dubiously. I tell her that when you're playing on one of the world's few moving, if not melting, courses, you just go with the floe.

The guides have brought two putters and two pitching wedges but only one ball. My twosome goes first. I chip, Daisy putts. To keep from falling over—a problem most golfers have only after visiting the 19th hole—I attach Yak-trax to my hiking boots. Unlike my daughter, I'm wearing so many layers of clothing, it's a wonder I can raise a club above shoulder height, let alone swing it.

The berg on Hole 2 is so tall, only a fly with crampons could climb to the top. I strike our ball and watch it rebound off the glistening slab and fall close to where the flag flutters in the middle of the green, or rather, white. But play can be rough on the smooth, as Daisy learns as she tries to putt off a film of snow. To get the backspin to make the ball stop, she must hit it cleanly, clipping the top. Alas, her clip is more of a clop, and the ball gets buried in a drift. When no one can find it, the game is put on ice.

On the final day, we ricochet off a refrigerator-size berg and veer within 30 feet of a pack-ice cathedral, whose two craggy pinnacles rise three stories from the bay. Suddenly, it crashes into the water with a thunderous splash. A small wave rocks our kayak. Where the cathedral once sat, a small chapel now bobs. Daisy's face turns a glacial white. "I've got goose bumps on my goose bumps," she says.

The close encounter doesn't cool Daisy's ardor for ice. She's got a big crush on a 50-foot slab in the shape of a golf bag. She suggests we lasso the berg and haul it ashore. By the time we get back to the airport, she reasons, it will have melted enough to strap a seat belt around. "Let it float," I advise. "That's not the only Ogio in the sea."

In fact, it's just the tip of the iceberg.

ACKNOWLEDGMENTS

For their greatly appreciated and timely generosity I wish to thank Rob Buchanan, Joel and Ethan Coen, Kris Dahl, Jaime Diaz, Dave Douglas, Georgia Getz, Jim Herre, Greg Kelly, John Papanek, Gil Rogin, Carl Schoettler, Michael Solomon, John Zorn, and the great Gogo Lidz—without whose encouragement this memoir would have been finished in half the time.

I wish to thank Daisy Lidz for her abiding patience and perspicacity.

My gratitude also goes, as ever, to Maggie Lidz, who saw some of these chapters early (and into light).

And for the lobster pot pies, Bonne Buche and chocolate-covered cream puffs: Bryan Sikora, Aimee Olexy, and Claire Shears.